the Diverticulitis
COOKBOOK
Feel Better, by Eating Better

100+ HEALTHY DELICIOUS RECIPES & 30 DAY MEAL PLAN

Written by Denalee Bell
Dietary Advice by Andrea Johnson

BONUSES

If you purchased this book from Amazon.com or other etailer, email info@diverticulitisdiet.com with your receipt number and bonuses will be emailed to you.

Bonuses include:

The Low-Residue Diet and Three-Day Meal Plan
Report on Diverticulitis Prevention Tactics
Lose Weight for Your Health

The Diverticulitis Cookbook: Feel Better, By Eating Better

Copyright © 2010 by Tiger Publishing, LLC. All rights reserved.

ISBN: 9781452825915

CONTENTS

Introduction

I remember the day my mom, Alice, called and said, "I'm in the hospital. Can you come?" Not words I've ever heard from my tough mom. After my father left her to raise me and my brother on our own when we were quite young, she became an independent business woman. She didn't have a formal education, but is an extremely intelligent woman with admirable ethics and old school ambition. She opened a café in the small town where we lived and provided my brother and me with a comfortable living. She worked 12-16 hours a day and somehow still made time for us. She took care of us, but also taught us to be independent and strong. She never whined or complained about her situation as a single mom, but made the best of it. In fact, I don't remember my mom ever complaining even after major surgery, a hysterectomy, or being poisoned, which, incidentally, left lifelong medical complications we are still finding out about.

Growing up with Alice, we didn't go to the doctor or hospital on a whim. There had better be a broken bone or bleeding to make a trip to Doc Howshar. So when I received her call, I didn't ask questions. I jumped in my car and raced to the hospital. When I got there, my tough mom looked broken. I could tell she was in excruciating pain as she lay wincing in the hospital bed. Tears were welling in her eyes (something else I had never seen) and her body was on fire with a high fever. I was baffled by her circumstances, and so were the doctors. She told us her pain was more painful than childbirth—I could relate to the pain of childbirth, but couldn't imagine anything worse than that.

My mom had already been diagnosed with diverticulosis before this trip to the hospital. She'd had minor flare-ups before, but did not associate this pain with her condition. Several hours and many tests later, the doctor diagnosed the episode as a diverticulitis attack. She was given pain medication, antibiotics, and a list of what not to eat to exacerbate her pain - specifically, she was not to eat nuts, seeds, popcorn and corn.

After that trip to the hospital, the attacks became more frequent and more severe over the next year. This was frustrating for my mother because she dutifully followed the doctor's instructions and quit eating all the trigger foods—nuts, seeds and popcorn. After several trips to the clinic and hospital and still not understanding the cause of her pain, I suggested she start a journal. She would document her eating habits and life events to see if we could find a connection with the flare-ups. We found some interesting factors preceding her flare-ups— high stress, bad eating habits (my determination, not hers) and an overall sedentary lifestyle.

I could not bear to see her in this kind of pain. So Mom and I began to research the condition thoroughly. I read every book I could get my hands on dealing with digestive issues, diverticulitis, and nutrition. Based on our research and trials and errors, we developed a plan to alleviate diverticulitis symptoms. There are several lifestyle changes that need to be addressed in preventing diverticulitis attacks. We found that reducing stress and changing to a high fiber, low-fat, low-sugar diet would be key in warding off future attacks. We asked Andrea Johnson, a respected registered dietician, to help us develop a meal plan and to edit our recipes.

Who Is Andrea Johnson?

Andrea Johnson, M.A., is a registered dietitian who currently blogs for a health supplement website, works with the local WIC nutrition program, and is an adjunct instructor for online nutrition courses at the University of Montana College of Technology in Missoula, MT. She built upon her experience as a dietitian as a clinical dietitian for three and a half years, building on her research skills there as well. During that time, she was published in the *Journal of Renal Nutrition* for her research on the effects of protein supplementation in dialysis patients. It was also during her clinical years that she developed a strong understanding of gastrointestinal disorders, which provided the ability to assist with editing the *Diverticulitis Digest Cookbook*.

Andrea has a Master's in Nutrition from Appalachian State University and a Bachelor's in Nutrition from the University of Tennessee in Knoxville. For the past 13 years, she has kept abreast of current research and continuing education, which has allowed her to provide the most up to date and reliable nutrition advice. Currently, she is working on becoming a certified LEAP therapist, allowing her to specialize in food allergies and sensitivities.

WHAT IS DIVERTICULITIS?

Diverticulitis is the result of a common condition known as diverticulosis. In diverticulosis, diverticula begin to form when the muscles of the colon wall work overtime to deal with hardened stools or lack of bulk in the diet. This results in small bulging pouches. Diverticulitis occurs when these pouches become inflamed or infected causing abdominal pain, fever, nausea, and changes in bowel routine. Infections typically arise when small bits of feces become trapped in the pockets as a result of constipation. Food can also become trapped. Both are wonderful breeding grounds for bacteria, which is the cause of infection and pain.

For those with diverticulosis, preventing a flare-up of symptoms is certainly the priority. Following a high fiber diet is not only imperative in preventing flare-ups, but also a good plan for overall digestive health. Mild cases of diverticulitis can also be treated with rest, diet changes and antibiotics.

What Causes Diverticulitis?

The exact cause of diverticular disease is still unresolved in the medical community. The scientific evidence suggests that our western diets—highly refined, processed and low in nutrients—and lack of exercise are largely to blame.

FIBER & MORE FIBER

Components of the diverticulitis diet include a low-residue, low-fiber diet during flare-ups. During a diverticulitis flare-up, you should remain on a low residue diet until symptoms subside. Pertinent recipes are listed the Low Residue chapter.

When symptoms improve, it's time to introduce a high fiber diet. A high fiber diet consists of 25 to 35 grams of fiber per day. You will need to slowly work up to a diet with this much fiber or you could stimulate a high amount of gas production that can lead to bloating and forceful diarrhea. It's always best to make gradual changes for fiber intake.

This fiber consists of both water soluble and water insoluble fibers. Insoluble fiber consists of the peels of fruits and vegetables and the husks of whole grains. Soluble fiber consists of gums, pectin and musilages that are found within fruit and vegetables. Oat bran and legumes are also considered to be soluble fiber.   When fiber is increased in the diet, it is also important to increase fluids. The daily recommendation of fiber, water, exercise, probiotics/prebiotics, omegas and a multivitamin/mineral supplement each day are also recommended to prevent diverticulitis flare-ups.

A WORD ON NUTS & SEEDS

For years, many diagnosed with diverticulosis were advised by their doctors to avoid all seeds and nuts, including foods with small seeds, such as tomatoes, cucumbers and strawberries. It was believed that these tiny particles could get lodged in the diverticula sacs, causing inflammation and possibly infection leading into diverticulitis. Recent studies have indicated there is **no scientific evidence that seeds and nuts** are the cause for diverticulitis flare-ups. We are learning that eating a high-fiber diet — which may include nuts and seeds — can actually reduce the risk of diverticular disease. In addition, all of these items become digested and soft by the time they reach the colon.

However, if you have an attack of diverticulitis and you believe that nuts and seeds triggered your attack, you may still have to stay away from the little culprits. Only you can tell the comfort level of your own body and just what it can handle. If you are prone to diverticulitis and are on a healthy upswing many doctors now believe it's okay to experiment with some seeds or nuts to find out whether or not your body can tolerate them and how much. As you experiment with the various nuts and seeds, take caution and try to chew them well.

However, don't forget that the most important part is to make sure you get enough fiber from other dietary sources.

How to Use This Cookbook and Meal Plan

Andrea Johnson and I prepared the recipes and meal plan in this cookbook together. Andrea's passion for nutrition and a healthy lifestyle were critical in developing these recipes and meal plan. The recipes and meal plan are meant to be used for a lifestyle change and not a temporary strategy to ward off pain.

Andrea created the high fiber meal plan ensuring an overall balanced diet with daily caloric intake as factors. Depending on your current lifestyle and caloric needs, you may lose weight on this meal plan. If losing weight is not a desired outcome for you, increase the amount of your servings at meal time or add a snack.

The meal plan is a guide for you and can be interchangeable with recipes from the cookbook. Not all recipes from the cookbook made it to the meal plan, but they do contain elements of a high fiber diet. Remember when interchanging recipes to include the correct amount of servings each day.

Ease into the 30 Day Meal Plan if you have not been consuming a diet including 25 grams a fiber a day. If you suddenly introduce a large amount of fiber to your diet, you may experience severe intestinal discomfort. Eat your normal diet and slowly incorporate the higher fiber recipes in this cookbook.

There are many more recipes beyond the meal plan in the cookbook. The meal plan is designed to help you develop a habit of eating a high fiber diet and eliminate the problem of deciding what to eat.

Busy Schedules

In today's society we are all busy, but it is most important to make this new lifestyle work for you. Keep it Simple! If you find you don't have time to cook every meal, there are quick high fiber meal replacement options for you. In addition, don't be afraid to use leftovers from dinner to lunch. The plan is flexible.

Meal Replacements

High protein/fiber meal replacement shakes or bars can be used to replace any meal or snack. My favorite meal replacements are Shakeology Meal Replacement Shakes. They have all natural ingredients and have digestive enzymes already in them without fillers (such as ash) found in other brands. Prebiotics are included. You can add more fiber to your shake, without affecting the taste, by throwing in a scoop of Shakeology Boost a fiber supplement that will pack in another 7 grams of fiber per serving.

On this program you may substitute one or two meals per day with Shakeology. If you are interested in losing weight, this product may help you. You can purchase or research this product at www.ShakeDirect.com

Using this cookbook and our suggested lifestyle changes, Andrea, Mom and I know you will feel better immediately and your life will be transformed by more energy too!

Bon Appétit!

Denalee Bell

30 Day Meal Plan

The 30 Day Meal Plan Guidelines: Eat 6 small meals per day. Include 30 grams of fiber. Servings: Breads 6 – 11 servings, Vegetables 3 – 5 servings, Fruit 2 -3 servings, Meat 2-3 servings/6 oz daily.

Day	Breakfast	Snack	Lunch	Snack	Dinner	Snack/ Dessert
1	Berry Barley Breakfast Or *Shakeology w/Fiber Boost	Apple slices	Sweet Cabbage Soup	Trail Mix	Shrimp Stir Fry	Raspberry Peach Crisp
2	Delicious Pancakes with 1 cup of fresh blueberries	Banana	Chicken Salad Nouveau Or *Shakeology w/Fiber Boost	Carrot Slices or Celery with Hummus	Maple Salmon Glazed Carrots	Apple Slices
3	Raspberry Smoothie	Avocado Slices	Thai Beef Salad Or *Shakeology w/Fiber	Baked Pita Chips, Jalapeno Hummus	Cinnamon Chicken Wild rice	Chocolate Chip Banana Bread Pudding
4	Bran Muffin	¾cup, Blueberries frozen or fresh with 4 oz. Cottage Cheese	Peanut Butter & Jelly on Whole Wheat, Grapes (1 handful)	*Shakeology w/Fiber Boost	Sausage Primavera Or *Shakeology w/Fiber Boost	Fall Fruit Salad
5	Hearty Southwest Omelet	Homemade Granola Bar	California Bean Sprout Salad	Celery with almond butter	Italian Sausage & Polenta	Apple Slices
6	Muesli Mix	Strawberries (1 cup)	Barley Casserole	Banana, yogurt	Sausage Soup w/Foil Wrapped Potatoes & Vegetables	Pear Bread Pudding
7	Breakfast Sausage Skillet	Healthy Banana Bread	5 Bean Salad & Tuna Sandwich	Fruit Smoothie	Salmon & Sweet Potatoes -½ Squash and ½ Zucchini fried in 1 Tbs butter w/garlic salt	Apple Slices

Day	Breakfast	Snack	Lunch	Snack	Dinner	Snack/ Dessert
8	Yogurt with Berries & Granola	Orange Slices	Roasted Asparagus Soup	Whole Wheat Crackers with Peanut Butter	Orange Chicken Brown Rice and Broccoli	Peanut Rounds Or *Shakeology With Fiber Boost
9	Whole Wheat Toast with Almond Butter	Avocado Slices	Foil-Wrapped Sweet Potatoes and Veggies	Trail Mix	Cilantro Chicken Succulent Spinach	Apple Slices
10	Breakfast Smoothie	Celery with Almond Butter	Pita Pockets Stuffed with vegetables & Chickpeas	Baked Pita Chips, Jalapeno Hummus	Roasted Pepper Pork & Potatoes w/ Asparagus grilled – spread oil on asparagus, add garlic salt and grill for 2-3 minutes.	Berries 'n' Cream
11	Orange Berry Oat Muffins	Grapefruit Slices	Tasty Tuna Sandwich	Homemade Granola Bar	Granny's Ham & Bean soup	Apple Slices
12	High fiber cereal such as Kashi Go Lean Crunch	Blueberries, frozen or fresh (1/2 c – 1c)	Hearty Minestrone Or *Shakeology w/Fiber Boost	Carrot Slices, Almonds (1 small handful)	Chicken Stir Fry Or *Shakeology w/Fiber Boost	ChocoRice Pudding
13	Blueberry Oatmeal Pancakes Or *Shakeology w/Fiber Boost	Homemade Granola Bar	Pita Pocket with Chickpeas and Vegetables	Whole Wheat Toast with Almond or Peanut Butter	Roasted Halibut with Spinach & Carrots	Apple Slices
14	Whole Grain Waffles		Butternut Squash Soup	Shakeology w/Fiber Boost	Greek Pasta w/Chicken	Apple Slices
15	Banana Strawberry Muffin Or *Shakeology w/Fiber Boost	Orange Slices	Hearty Minestrone Soup, ½ Tuna Salad Sandwich on Wheat Bread, Fresh berries		Grilled Cherry Pork Chop, Cooked Broccoli (1 c)	Baked Pears with Cranberries

*Shakeology w/ Fiber Boost will give you a boost of 10 grams of fiber per serving. See www.ShakeDirect.com for more information.

Day	Breakfast	Snack	Lunch	Snack	Dinner	Snack/ Dessert
16	2/3 cup Oatmeal with ½ cup Banana Slices 1 cup Nonfat Milk	Strawberries (1 cup)	Easy Reuben	Great Guacamole with Guiltless Chips	Yummy Black Bean Burrito with Baked Pita Chips	Apple slices
17	Yogurt with Berries & Granola	Cottage Cheese Stuffed Celery	Chicken Wrap Or *Shakeology w/Fiber Boost	2 Wasa™ brand Crackers w/ Cream Cheese & Sliced Kiwi Fruit	Roast Pork & Potatoes Broccoli with Garlic Sauce	Apple slices
18	Breakfast Sausage Skillet	Pear Slices	Beef Barley Soup	Baked Pita Chips, Jalapeno Hummus	Whole Wheat Linguine with Bacon & Baby Spinach	Apple slices
19	High fiber cereal, such as Kashi Go Lean Crunch	Easy Edamame	Peanut Butter & Jelly on Whole Wheat, Grapes (1 handful)	Green Apple with Peanut or Almond Butter	Baked Halibut with Orzo and Grilled Asparagus	Whole Grain Cereal with 8 oz Skim Milk
20	Omelet Eggstraordinaire	Healthy Banana Bread	Pita Pockets Stuffed with Vegetables & Chickpeas	Great Guacamole with Guiltless Chips	Sweet Potato Burrito with Mango Salsa, Guiltless Chips, Guacamole	Apple Slices
21	Banana Strawberry Muffins	Apple Slices with Peanut Butter	Tasty Tuna Sandwich	Fruit Smoothie	White Chicken Chili, Guiltless Chips	Chocolate PB Bars
22	Breakfast Sausage Skillet	Apple Slices	Breaded Artichoke Bites	Trail Mix	Fresh Broccoli and Beef Stir Fry	
23	Bran Muffins	Blueberries, frozen or fresh (1/2 c – 1c)	Lentil Soup Or *Shakeology w/Fiber Boost	Easy Edamame	Balsamic Buttered Tilapia with Asparagus	Apple Slices
24	Granola, Yogurt & Fruit Parfait	Orange Slices	*Shakeology w/Fiber Boost	Baked Pita Chips, Black Bean Dip	Fresh Fajitas with Baked Pita Chips	Healthy Banana Bread

*Shakeology w/ Fiber Boost will give you a boost of 10 grams of fiber per serving. See www.ShakeDirect.com for more information.

Day	Breakfast	Snack	Lunch	Snack	Dinner	Snack/ Dessert
25	Orange Berry Oat Muffins	Blueberries, frozen or fresh (1/2 c – 1c)	Hearty Minestrone Soup, ½ Tuna Salad Sandwich on Wheat Bread, Fresh Berries	Yogurt with Fruit Or *Shakeology w/Fiber Boost	Black Beans with Pepper and Cumin Vinaigrette, Guiltless Chips	Chocolate PB Bars
26	Oatmeal with Fruit	Celery with wedge of Laughing Cow Swiss Cheese	Tortilla Wrap	Whole wheat Toast with Almond Butter	Fish Tacos	Apple Slices
27	Berry Barley Breakfast	Pear Slices	Lentil Soup	Carrot and celery with hummus	Crab Quiche	*Shakeology w/Fiber Boost
28	Yogurt with Fruit & Granola Parfait	Celery and 1 Tbs Peanut Butter	Peanut Butter & Jelly on Whole Wheat, Grapes (1 handful)	Easy Edamame	Corn Chowder	Oatmeal PB cookies
29	Whole Grain Waffles	Grapefruit Slices	Pita Pockets Stuffed with vegetables & Chickpeas	2 Wasa™ brand Crackers with Peanut Butter	Chicken Sherry , Succulent Spinach, Garlic Potatoes	Apple Slices
30	Raspberry Banana Smoothie	Homemade Granola Bar	Granny's Ham & Bean Soup	Baked Pita Chips, Black Bean Dip	Orange Roughy Parmesan, Wild Rice	Oatmeal PB cookies

*Shakeology w/ Fiber Boost will give you a boost of 10 grams of fiber per serving. See www.ShakeDirect.com for more information.

Appetizers & Snacks

Snacks are a great way to sneak in extra fiber and other important nutrients into your diet. A healthy snack will help satisfy hunger and prevent overeating during meal times that can lead to digestive irritation.

> You better cut the pizza in four pieces, because
> I'm not hungry enough to eat six.
> ~Yogi Berra

Baked Pita Chips

Great high fiber snack for any dip or spread. This is great with hummus or salsa.

4 pieces whole wheat pita bread

Procedure

1. Preheat oven to 400°.
2. Separate each piece of pita bread by cutting the edge. Cut each layer into 8 wedges.
3. Place wedges in single layer on two ungreased cookie sheets.
4. Bake for 9-10 minutes or until crisp and golden brown. Cool and enjoy.

Servings: 4

Nutrition Facts

Percent daily values based on the Reference Daily Intake (RDI) for a 2000 calorie diet.
Nutrition information calculated from recipe ingredients.

Amount Per Serving	
Calories	170.24
Calories From Fat (8%)	13.97
	% Daily Value
Total Fat 1.66g	**3%**
Saturated Fat 0.26g	1%
Cholesterol 0mg	**0%**
Sodium 340.48mg	**14%**
Potassium 108.8mg	**3%**
Total Carbohydrates 35.2g	**12%**
Fiber 4.74g	19%
Sugar 0.52g	
Protein 6.27g	**13%**

Black Bean Dip

Great with baked pita chips, spicy tortilla chips or raw vegetables.

2	Tbs	canned chopped green chilies	1/2 cup	plain yogurt
1		small onion chopped	1/2 tsp	ground cumin
2		cloves garlic, crushed	1/4 tsp	salt
1		15-ounce can black beans, rinsed and drained		

Procedure

1. In blender or food processor, combine all ingredients and blend until smooth.
2. Serve with baked pita chips, tortilla chips or fresh assorted raw vegetables.

Servings: 4

Nutrition Facts

Percent daily values based on the Reference Daily Intake (RDI) for a 2000 calorie diet.
Nutrition information calculated from recipe ingredients.

Amount Per Serving	
Calories	118.85
Calories From Fat (13%)	15.87
	% Daily Value
Total Fat 0.95g	1%
Saturated Fat 0.32g	2%
Cholesterol 1.87mg	<1%
Sodium 523.19mg	22%
Potassium 131.26mg	4%
Total Carbohydrates 6.06g	2%
Fiber 5.81g	23%
Sugar 2.08g	
Protein 8.06g	16%

Breaded Artichoke Bites

Artichoke lovers beware—you will become addicted to these!

2	6.5-ounce jars marinated artichoke hearts, chopped		1/8 tsp	ground black pepper
1	small onion, chopped		1/8 tsp	dried oregano
1	clove garlic, minced		1/8 tsp	hot pepper sauce
4	eggs, beaten		2 cups	shredded sharp cheddar cheese
1/4 cup	fine dry bread crumbs		2 Tbs	finely minced fresh parsley
1/2 tsp	sea salt			

Procedure

1. Preheat oven to 325°. Grease muffin pan or place baking cups in mini muffin baking pan.
2. Drain marinade from 1 jar of artichokes into a medium skillet. Drain second jar and discard marinade. Heat the marinade in the medium skillet. Add the onions and garlic and sauté' until onion is tender, about 3-4 minutes.
3. In a medium bowl, combine the eggs, bread crumbs, salt, pepper, oregano and hot pepper sauce. Slowly mix in the shredded cheddar cheese, parsley and artichoke hearts. Blend the marinade with the sautéed onions and garlic into the mix.
4. Place ingredients from the contents of the bowl into individual muffin spots. Bake for approximately 30 minutes and allow muffins to cool briefly. Cut into one-inch squares and serve.

Servings: 12

Nutrition Facts

Percent daily values based on the Reference Daily Intake (RDI) for a 2000 calorie diet.
Nutrition information calculated from recipe ingredients.

Amount Per Serving	
Calories	132.53
Calories From Fat (56%)	73.74
	% Daily Value
Total Fat 8.34g	13%
Saturated Fat 4.6g	23%
Cholesterol 101.56mg	34%
Sodium 272.1mg	11%
Potassium 178.09mg	5%
Total Carbohydrates 6.35g	2%
Fiber 1.99g	8%
Sugar 0.61g	
Protein 8.66g	17%

Crunchy Cherry Party Mix

4	cups	bite-size corn or rice square cereal (such as Corn or Rice Chex)	3	Tbs	margarine or butter, melted
2	cups	bite-size wheat square cereal (such as Wheat Chex)	1	Tbs	Worcestershire sauce
			2	tsp	chili powder
			1/4 tsp		garlic powder
2	cups	broken whole grain Melba toast	1/4 tsp		onion powder
			1/8 tsp		ground red pepper
2	cups	small fat-free pretzel twists	1-1/2	cups	dried tart cherries

Procedure

1. Preheat oven to 300°F. Put corn or rice cereal, wheat cereal, Melba toast and pretzels in a large bowl; stir to mix. In a glass measuring cup or small bowl, stir together melted margarine or butter, Worcestershire sauce, chili powder, garlic powder, onion powder and ground red pepper. Drizzle over cereal mixture. Toss to coat.

2. Spread cereal mixture in a 15x10x1-inch (or a 13x9x2-inch) baking pan. Bake about 25 minutes, stirring every 7 to 8 minutes. Remove from oven; stir in dried cherries.

3. Pour onto aluminum foil to cool completely. Store in a tightly covered container for up to 1 week.

Servings: 20

Nutrition Facts

Serving size: 1/20 of a recipe (2.5 ounces).
Percent daily values based on the Reference Daily Intake (RDI) for a 2000 calorie diet.
Nutrition information calculated from recipe ingredients.

Amount Per Serving	
Calories	262.94
Calories From Fat (11%)	29.33
	% Daily Value
Total Fat 3.37g	5%
Saturated Fat 0.89g	4%
Cholesterol 1.87mg	<1%
Sodium 682.7mg	28%
Potassium 103.61mg	3%
Total Carbohydrates 53.71g	18%
Fiber 3.71g	15%
Sugar 1.63g	
Protein 6.06g	12%

Great Guacamole

Avocados are a great source of fiber and have other great health benefits such as lowering your cholesterol and helping your body to absorb other nutrients more efficiently.

3	avocados, peeled, pitted and mashed	3 Tbs	chopped fresh cilantro
1	lime, juiced	2	roma tomatoes, seeded and chopped
1 tsp	salt	1 tsp	minced garlic
1/2 cup	diced onions	1 pinch	ground cayenne pepper

Procedure

1. In a bowl, combine all of the ingredients.
2. Serve with baked pita chips or tortilla chips.

Servings: 4

Nutrition Facts

Percent daily values based on the Reference Daily Intake (RDI) for a 2000 calorie diet.
Nutrition information calculated from recipe ingredients.

Amount Per Serving	
Calories	258.9
Calories From Fat (68%)	177.21
	% Daily Value
Total Fat 21.52g	33%
Saturated Fat 2.77g	14%
Cholesterol 0mg	0%
Sodium 609.33mg	25%
Potassium 719.6mg	21%
Total Carbohydrates 20.33g	7%
Fiber 10.74g	43%
Sugar 4.36g	
Protein 4.36g	9%

Guiltless Chips

2	Tbs	butter, melted	8		corn tortillas
1/2 tsp	chili powder				

Procedure

1. Preheat oven to 400°. Mix melted butter and chili powder in a small bowl. Brush on one side of tortillas.
2. Cut each tortilla into 6 to 8 wedges. Place in 2 ungreased 15 ½x10½x1" jelly roll pans.
3. Bake uncovered 8 to 10 minutes or until crisp and golden brown; cool.

Servings: 12

Nutrition Facts

Percent daily values based on the Reference Daily Intake (RDI) for a 2000 calorie diet.
Nutrition information calculated from recipe ingredients.

Amount Per Serving	
Calories	55.79
Calories From Fat (37%)	20.66
	% Daily Value
Total Fat 2.37g	4%
Saturated Fat 1.28g	6%
Cholesterol 5.09mg	2%
Sodium 3.26mg	<1%
Potassium 29.34mg	<1%
Total Carbohydrates 8.14g	3%
Fiber 0.94g	4%
Sugar 0.01g	
Protein 1.02g	2%

Healthy High-Fiber Trail Mix

Quick snack you can much on or even eat for breakfast.

| 1 | cup | low fat granola or homemade granola (see recipe on following page) |
| 4 | cups | mixed high fiber cereal — pick a few that you like (Kashi©, Barbara's Shredded Spoonfuls®) |

| 1 | cup | dried raisins or cranberries |
| 1/2 cup | | chopped nuts, *optional* |

Procedure

Mix all ingredients and place into an airtight container. This will keep for a few weeks.

Nutrition Facts

Percent daily values based on the Reference Daily Intake (RDI) for a 2000 calorie diet.
Nutrition information calculated from recipe ingredients.

Amount Per Serving	
Calories	395.57
Calories From Fat (20%)	80.31
	% Daily Value
Total Fat 9.55g	15%
Saturated Fat 0.97g	5%
Cholesterol 0mg	0%
Sodium 13.89mg	<1%
Potassium 261.43mg	7%
Total Carbohydrates 73.75g	25%
Fiber 5.21g	21%
Sugar 26.46g	
Protein 9.99g	20%

Homemade Granola

For snack or recipe on preceding page.

If you are sensitive to nuts, substitute cereal such as corn flakes or puffed rice for the nuts.

1	cup	brown sugar
½	cup	water
1	Tbs	vanilla extract
8	cups	rolled oats
1 ½	cups	chopped nuts (walnuts, pecans, almonds)
1/3	cup	dried cranberries

Procedure

1. Preheat oven to 275°. Prepare 2 large baking sheets with parchment paper.
2. In a microwave proof bowl, combine brown sugar and water. Microwave on high for approximately 5 minutes, until sugar is dissolved. Mix in vanilla and salt.
3. In a large bowl combine oats, nuts, dried cranberries and brown sugar mixture, mixing until well coated.
4. Spread mixture on both sheets and bake for 45 minutes to 1 hour. Cool completely and store in an airtight container.

Servings: 10

Jalapeno Hummus

Serve with Baked Pita Chips or fresh veggies. Tahini is the key to a good hummus. You can find it at most supermarkets or health food stores. I found it in the Asian section at our supermarket.

1	cup	garbanzo beans
1/3 cup		canned jalapeno pepper slices, juice reserved, seeds removed
3	Tbs	tahini
3		cloves garlic, minced

2	Tbs	lemon juice
1/2 tsp		ground cumin
1/2 tsp		curry powder
		crushed red pepper to taste

Procedure

1. In a blender or food processor, mix garbanzo beans, jalapeno peppers and reserved juice, tahini, garlic, and lemon juice. Season with cumin, curry powder and crushed red pepper. Blend until smooth.

Servings: 4

Nutrition Facts

Serving size: 1/4 of a recipe (3.3 ounces).
Percent daily values based on the Reference Daily Intake (RDI) for a 2000 calorie diet.
Nutrition information calculated from recipe ingredients.

Amount Per Serving	
Calories	148.09
Calories From Fat (39%)	57.44
	% Daily Value
Total Fat 6.86g	11%
Saturated Fat 0.93g	5%
Cholesterol 0mg	0%
Sodium 371.85mg	15%
Potassium 203.52mg	6%
Total Carbohydrates 18.19g	6%
Fiber 3.65g	15%
Sugar 0.46g	
Protein 5.28g	11%

Breakfast

Breakfast is the most important meal of the day. Start your day off right with a nutritious breakfast to give you energy and the nutrients you need to stay healthy. If you find you are pressed for time in the morning, many of the breakfast recipes can be made ahead and frozen, especially the muffins.

"Eat breakfast like a king,
lunch like a prince,
and dinner like a pauper"

~Adelle Davis

Berry Barley Breakfast

This recipe will stay good in the refrigerator for 5-7 days. Mix with vanilla yogurt for a great treat!

1/2 cup	barley	1-1/2	cups	fresh raspberries
6	cups water	1/2 cup	raisins
1/2 cup	granulated sugar	1	cup	pitted cherries

Procedure

1. In a large bowl, soak the barley in the water overnight; do not drain.
2. In a large saucepan over low heat, simmer the barley for one hour. Then add the sugar, raspberries and raisins and simmer for another 30 minutes. Add the cherries and simmer for another 15 minutes, or until the soup becomes relatively thick. Allow to chill in the refrigerator and serve cold.

Servings: 6

Nutrition Facts

Serving size: 1/6 of a recipe (11.9 ounces).
Percent daily values based on the Reference Daily Intake (RDI) for a 2000 calorie diet.
Nutrition information calculated from recipe ingredients.

Amount Per Serving	
Calories	255.88
Calories From Fat (3%)	7.89
	% Daily Value
Total Fat 0.94g	1%
Saturated Fat 0.09g	<1%
Cholesterol 0mg	0%
Sodium 11.73mg	<1%
Potassium 219.06mg	6%
Total Carbohydrates 62.48g	21%
Fiber 6.49g	26%
Sugar 26.27g	
Protein 3.36g	7%

Blueberry Oatcakes

Take the preservatives out of your breakfast with this healthy pancake alternative.

1/2 cup	whole wheat flour
1/2 cup	all-purpose flour
2 Tbs	brown sugar
2 Tbs	baking powder
3/4 tsp	salt
1 1/2 cups	quick cooking oats
2 cups	soy milk (may substitute buttermilk or evaporated milk)
3	eggs, beaten
1/4 cup	olive oil (may substitute applesauce)
1/2 cup	frozen blueberries

Procedure

1. Preheat a lightly oiled griddle over medium heat.
2. In a large bowl, mix whole wheat flour, all-purpose flour, brown sugar, baking powder and salt. In a small bowl, mix oats and soy milk. Whisk in eggs and olive oil. Pour into the flour mixture all at once.
3. Continue mixing until smooth. Gently fold in blueberries.
4. Pour batter about 1/4 cup at a time onto the prepared griddle. Cook 1 to 2 minutes, until bubbly. Flip and continue cooking until lightly browned.

Servings: 8
Nutrition Facts
Serving size: 1/8 of a recipe (4.9 ounces).
Percent daily values based on the Reference Daily Intake (RDI) for a 2000 calorie diet.
Nutrition information calculated from recipe ingredients.

Amount Per Serving	
Calories	255.75
Calories From Fat (39%)	99.67
	% Daily Value
Total Fat 11.33g	17%
Saturated Fat 1.92g	10%
Cholesterol 92mg	31%
Sodium 650.25mg	27%
Potassium 193.44mg	6%
Total Carbohydrates 30.82g	10%
Fiber 2.9g	12%
Sugar 4.85g	
Protein 9.19g	18%

Bran Muffins

1 ½	cups	whole wheat flour	¾	cup	skim milk
¾	cup	ground flaxseed	2		eggs, beaten
¾	cup	oat bran	1	tsp	vanilla
1	cup	brown sugar	2	Tbs	vegetable oil
2	tsp	baking soda	2	cups	carrots, shredded
1	tsp	baking powder	2		apples, peeled and shredded
1	tsp	salt			
2	tsp	ground cinnamon	½	cup	raisins

Procedure

1. Preheat oven to 350°. Grease muffin pan or line with paper muffin liners.
   Since cleanup isn't my favorite pastime, I usually choose the cupcake/muffin liners.
2. In a large bowl, mix together flour, flaxseed, oat bran, brown sugar, baking soda, baking powder, salt and cinnamon. In a separate bowl, combine milk, eggs, vanilla and oil. Combine the dry and wet ingredients until just blended. Stir in the carrots, apples, raisins and nuts. Fill prepared muffin cups 2/3 full with batter.
3. Bake at 350° for 15 to 20 minutes, or until a toothpick inserted into the center of a muffin comes out clean.

Servings: 15

Nutrition Facts

Serving size: 1/15 of a recipe.
Percent daily values based on the Reference Daily Intake (RDI) for a 2000 calorie diet.
Nutrition information provided by the recipe author.

Amount Per Serving	
Calories	335.95
Calories From Fat (51%)	171.2
	% Daily Value
Total Fat 19.95g	31%
Saturated Fat 2.83g	14%
Cholesterol 36.94mg	12%
Sodium 393.8mg	16%
Potassium 270.52mg	8%
Total Carbohydrates 35.67g	12%
Fiber 2.71g	11%
Sugar 18.87g	
Protein 7.35g	15%

Breakfast Sausage Skillet

This recipe will work for breakfast, lunch or dinner. You can substitute the turkey sausage for regular sausage. We suggest turkey kielbasa to keep calories and fat to a minimum.

6		red potatoes, cubed		1	Tbs	paprika
1	lb	turkey kielbasa sausage		2	tsp	onion powder
2	Tbs	olive oil		2	tsp	garlic powder
1-1/2	tsp	salt		6		eggs, beaten
1/2 tsp		pepper				

Procedure

1. Preheat oven to 375°.
2. Place potatoes in a saucepan with enough water to cover. Bring to a boil and cook over medium heat until tender, about 10 minutes. Drain.
3. While the potatoes are cooking, brown the sausage in a large skillet over medium-high heat. Once the skin is browned, cut into 2-inch pieces.
4. Transfer the potatoes and sausage to a 9x13 inch baking dish. Drizzle the olive oil over them, and season with salt, pepper, garlic powder, onion powder and paprika.
5. Bake for 15 minutes in preheated oven. While the sausage and potatoes are baking, reheat the same skillet with the sausage juices over medium heat. Pour in beaten eggs, and cook, stirring occasionally, until eggs are scrambled and cooked through. Stir into the sausage and potatoes before serving.

Servings: 5

Nutrition Facts

Serving size: 1/5 of a recipe
Percent daily values based on the Reference Daily Intake (RDI) for a 2000 calorie diet.
Nutrition information calculated from recipe ingredients.

Amount Per Serving	
Calories	376.57
Calories From Fat (41%)	152.68
	% Daily Value
Total Fat 16.56g	25%
Saturated Fat 4.26g	21%
Cholesterol 342.88mg	114%
Sodium 1601.96mg	67%
Potassium 931.93mg	27%
Total Carbohydrates 29.27g	10%
Fiber 3.08g	12%
Sugar 1.22g	
Protein 25.65g	51%

Breakfast Smoothie

1	frozen	banana	1	tsp	vanilla
½	cup	soy milk	1	cup	plain yogurt
¼	cup	old fashioned oats	5		strawberries

Procedure

1. In a blender, combine all ingredients until smooth. Enjoy!

Servings: 2

Nutrition Facts

Serving size: 1/2 of a recipe
Percent daily values based on the Reference Daily Intake (RDI) for a 2000 calorie diet.
Nutrition information calculated from recipe ingredients.

Amount Per Serving	
Calories	267.3
Calories From Fat (14%)	37.32
	% Daily Value
Total Fat 4.21g	6%
Saturated Fat 1.61g	8%
Cholesterol 7.47mg	2%
Sodium 111.87mg	5%
Potassium 851.89mg	24%
Total Carbohydrates 48.61g	16%
Fiber 5.28g	21%
Sugar 17.65g	
Protein 11.2g	22%

Delicious Oat-Wheat Pancakes

1 ½ cups	old fashioned oats		1	cup	milk
1 ½ cups	whole wheat flour		¼	cup	vegetable oil
½ cup	wheat germ		2		eggs
2 tsp	baking soda		1/3 cup		sugar
1 tsp	baking powder		1	tsp	vanilla
½ tsp	salt		1	dash	cinnamon
1 ½ cups	buttermilk				

Procedure

1. Grind oats in a food processor or blender until fine. In a large bowl, combine the ground oats, flour, wheat germ, baking soda, baking powder and salt.

2. In a separate bowl, mix buttermilk, milk, oil, eggs, sugar, vanilla and cinnamon with an electric mixer until smooth. Mix wet ingredients into dry with a few swift strokes. Do not over mix.

3. Preheat a skillet to medium with 1-2 tablespoons oil. Pour 1/3 cup of batter on the skillet. When light brown, flip.

Servings: 5

Nutrition Facts

Serving size: 1/5 of a recipe
Percent daily values based on the Reference Daily Intake (RDI) for a 2000 calorie diet.
Nutrition information calculated from recipe ingredients.

Amount Per Serving	
Calories	497.24
Calories From Fat (31%)	155.04
	% Daily Value
Total Fat 17.62g	**27%**
Saturated Fat 2.93g	**15%**
Cholesterol 91.44mg	**30%**
Sodium 960.11mg	**40%**
Potassium 362.69mg	**10%**
Total Carbohydrates 69.43g	**23%**
Fiber 4.62g	**18%**
Sugar 20.27g	
Protein 16.58g	**33%**

Hearty Southwestern Omelet

Serve with sour cream and guacamole.

1	15- to 15 1/2-ounce can black beans, rinsed, drained		1/2	red bell pepper, cut into strips
3/4 cup	purchased tomatillo salsa		2 cups	sliced mushrooms (about 5 ounces)
4	large eggs		1/2 cup	red onions
2	green onions, chopped		1 cup	(packed) coarsely grated Monterey Jack cheese (about 4 ounces)
1/4 tsp	salt		3 Tbs	chopped fresh cilantro
1/4 tsp	ground black pepper			
3 Tbs	butter, divided			

Procedure

1. Stir black beans and tomatillo salsa in a medium saucepan over medium heat until heated through. Remove bean and salsa mixture from heat. Cover and keep warm while preparing omelet.

2. Whisk eggs, green onions, salt and ground black pepper in medium bowl to blend. Melt 2 tablespoons butter in medium nonstick skillet over medium heat. Add bell pepper and sliced mushrooms to skillet; stir until mushrooms are brown, about 8 minutes. Transfer vegetables to bowl.

3. Melt remaining 1 tablespoon butter in same skillet over medium heat. Add egg mixture. Cook without stirring until beginning to set, about 4 minutes. Sprinkle with vegetables, Jack cheese and 1 tablespoon chopped cilantro. Cover skillet and cook until cheese melts and eggs are set, about 2 minutes. Slide large spatula under omelet to loosen. Fold omelet in half; turn out onto platter. Top omelet with bean and salsa mixture. Sprinkle with remaining 2 tablespoons chopped cilantro and serve.
    Servings: 3

Nutrition Facts

Serving size: 1/3 of a recipe
Percent daily values based on the Reference Daily Intake (RDI) for a 2000 calorie diet.
Nutrition information calculated from recipe ingredients.

Amount Per Serving	
Calories	556.1
Calories From Fat (44%)	247.09
	% Daily Value
Total Fat 27.99g	**43%**
Saturated Fat 14.73g	**74%**
Cholesterol 381.12mg	**127%**
Sodium 1233.75mg	**51%**
Potassium 1087.87mg	**31%**
Total Carbohydrates 44.38g	**15%**
Fiber 15.2g	**61%**
Sugar 4.87g	
Protein 34.8g	**70%**

Homemade Granola Bars

2	cups	oats	½	cup	honey
3/4 cup		wheat germ	4	Tbs	butter
3/4 cup		sunflower seeds	2	tsp	vanilla extract
1	cup	peanuts, crushed	½	tsp	kosher salt
2/3 cup		brown sugar	1	cup	dried fruit

Procedure

1. Preheat oven to 400°. Mix oats, wheat germ, sunflower seeds and crushed peanuts in a baking dish with sides. Toast mixture in the oven for 10 to 12 minutes, stirring every few minutes so the mixture doesn't burn.

2. Meanwhile, prepare an 11x13 inch glass baking dish by lining it with waxed paper lightly sprayed with nonstick spray.

3. In a saucepan simmer brown sugar, honey, butter, vanilla and salt. Stir constantly.

4. In a large bowl combine toasted mixture and contents of saucepan.

5. Dump granola mixture into prepared baking dish. Spread mixture with a wooden spoon or spatula. Fold over the sides of the waxed paper or add a sheet on top. Press the granola firmly and compact. Cool for 2 to 3 hours.

6. Open the waxed paper. Carefully turn the granola onto a large cutting board, peeling away the rest of the paper. Pressing with a big knife, cut granola into the size of your choosing. Store in airtight container or cover in plastic wrap.

Servings: 20

Nutrition Facts

Serving size: 1/20 of a recipe
Percent daily values based on the Reference Daily Intake (RDI) for a 2000 calorie diet.
Nutrition information calculated from recipe ingredients.

Amount Per Serving	
Calories	206.76
Calories From Fat (34%)	69.76
	% Daily Value
Total Fat 8.24g	13%
Saturated Fat 2.31g	12%
Cholesterol 6.11mg	2%
Sodium 51.58mg	2%
Potassium 214.59mg	6%
Total Carbohydrates 29.49g	10%
Fiber 3.07g	12%
Sugar 15.21g	
Protein 6.07g	12%

Morning Magic Muffins

The consistency of Morning Magic Muffins is heartier than a traditional muffin.
Tip: Make a couple of batches, allow to cool then freeze.

1	cup	all-purpose flour	1		egg
1	cup	whole wheat flour	1/2 cup		unsweetened applesauce
3/4 cup		ground flaxseed	1/3 cup		orange juice
3/4 cup		sugar	1/4 cup		canola oil
2 3/4	tsp	baking powder	2	tsp	vanilla extract
2	tsp	ground cinnamon	2	cups	grated carrots
3/4 tsp		salt	1/2 cup		flaked coconut
1/4 tsp		baking soda	1/2 cup		raisins
4		egg whites	1		medium tart apple, peeled and grated

Procedure

1. Preheat oven to 350°.
2. In a large bowl combine all-purpose flour, whole wheat flour, ground flaxseed, sugar, baking powder, ground cinnamon, salt and baking soda. In another bowl, beat the egg whites, egg, applesauce, orange juice, oil and vanilla. Stir into dry ingredients just until moistened. Be careful not to over-stir. Fold in the carrots, coconut, raisins and apple.
3. Spray muffin cups with nonstick cooking spray or use baking liners. Fill cups 3/4 full.
4. Bake 15-18 minutes or until a toothpick comes out clean.
5. Cool for 5 minutes before removing from pans to wire racks.

Servings: 18
Nutrition Facts
Serving size: 1/18 of a recipe
Percent daily values based on the Reference Daily Intake (RDI) for a 2000 calorie diet.
Nutrition information calculated from recipe ingredients.

Amount Per Serving	
Calories	251.11
Calories From Fat (47%)	118.53
	% Daily Value
Total Fat 13.45g	21%
Saturated Fat 1.82g	9%
Cholesterol 11.75mg	4%
Sodium 227.94mg	9%
Potassium 161.84mg	5%
Total Carbohydrates 30.32g	10%
Fiber 1.33g	5%
Sugar 14.93g	
Protein 3.21g	6%

Muesli Mix

3	cups	puffed rice	½	cup	almonds
1	cup	organic brown rice dry cereal	1	cup	sunflower seeds
3	cups	organic corn flakes	1	cup	dried cranberries
1	cup	roasted soy nuts	1	cup	dried dates

Procedure

1. Mix all of the ingredients together and store in airtight container.
2. Enjoy by itself or with milk or yogurt and berries.

Servings: 10

Nutrition Facts

Serving size: 1/10 of a recipe
Percent daily values based on the Reference Daily Intake (RDI) for a 2000 calorie diet.
Nutrition information calculated from recipe ingredients.

Amount Per Serving	
Calories	457.21
Calories From Fat (20%)	91.07
	% Daily Value
Total Fat 10.8g	17%
Saturated Fat 0.55g	3%
Cholesterol 0mg	0%
Sodium 4mg	<1%
Potassium 245.29mg	7%
Total Carbohydrates 82.98g	28%
Fiber 8.37g	33%
Sugar 12.48g	
Protein 10.88g	22%

Omelet Eggstraordinaire

Omelet for One.

2		eggs	1/4 cup	prepared salsa
1	tsp	garlic, diced	1/8 cup	red onion
1/2 Tbs		canola oil	1/8 cup	green bell peppers
1/2 tsp		salt	1/8 cup	sweet red pepper
1/2 tsp		black pepper	1/8 cup	tomato, diced
2		button mushrooms, sliced	2 Tbs	olive oil, extra virgin

Procedure

1. Sauté red onion, red and green peppers, and tomato in olive oil and garlic.
2. Add salt and pepper
3. Break eggs and mix in bowl.
4. Add egg mixture to cooked vegetables. Cook until set. Flip and finish cooking to desired doneness and fold onto plate. Top with salsa.

Servings: 1

Nutrition Facts

Serving size: Entire recipe
Percent daily values based on the Reference Daily Intake (RDI) for a 2000 calorie diet.
Nutrition information calculated from recipe ingredients.

Amount Per Serving	
Calories	457.94
Calories From Fat (76%)	345.91

	% Daily Value
Total Fat 38.94g	**60%**
Saturated Fat 7.3g	**37%**
Cholesterol 490.68mg	**164%**
Sodium 1719.28mg	**72%**
Potassium 594.7mg	**17%**
Total Carbohydrates 11.27g	**4%**
Fiber 2.81g	**11%**
Sugar 4.72g	
Protein 17.86g	**36%**

Orange Berry-Oat Muffins

½	cup	rolled oats		1	medium	orange
½	cup	lowfat buttermilk		½	cup	sugar
1 ½	cups	whole wheat flour		¼	cup	canola oil
1	tsp	baking powder		1		egg
½	tsp	baking soda		1	cup	blueberries
½	tsp	ground cinnamon		½	cup	dried cranberries
¼	tsp	salt				

Procedure

1. Preheat oven to 400°. Stir together oats and buttermilk in a small bowl and set aside for 5 minutes.

2. Combine whole wheat flour, baking powder, baking soda, cinnamon and salt together in a medium bowl. Grate rind from orange and add to a large bowl; squeeze 1/2 cup orange juice and add to rind. Whisk in sugar, oil and egg until mixture is smooth. Blend in oatmeal mixture, followed by flour mixture. Stir until ingredients are just combined, then gently fold in berries.

3. Spoon batter into prepared muffin tins and bake for 15 minutes or until a toothpick inserted in center of muffin comes out clean.   Servings: 12

Nutrition Facts

Serving size: 1/12 of a recipe (3.5 ounces).
Percent daily values based on the Reference Daily Intake (RDI) for a 2000 calorie diet.
Nutrition information calculated from recipe ingredients.

Amount Per Serving	
Calories	244.57
Calories From Fat (22%)	53.78
	% Daily Value
Total Fat 6.09g	9%
Saturated Fat 0.62g	3%
Cholesterol 20.85mg	7%
Sodium 160.93mg	7%
Potassium 123.51mg	4%
Total Carbohydrates 45.66g	15%
Fiber 4.37g	17%
Sugar 11.19g	
Protein 3.62g	7%

Raspberry Banana Smoothie

½	cup	fresh raspberries	1	cup	vanilla low fat yogurt
½		banana	1	tsp	honey
½	cup	skim milk or soy milk			

Procedure

1. Combine all ingredients in a food processor and mix until desired consistency.

Servings: 1

Nutrition Facts

Serving size: Entire recipe (15.8 ounces).
Percent daily values based on the Reference Daily Intake (RDI) for a 2000 calorie diet.
Nutrition information calculated from recipe ingredients.

Amount Per Serving	
Calories	489.67
Calories From Fat (25%)	124.25
	% Daily Value
Total Fat 14.19g	22%
Saturated Fat 8.74g	44%
Cholesterol 54.49mg	18%
Sodium 571.82mg	24%
Potassium 931.94mg	27%
Total Carbohydrates 64.28g	21%
Fiber 5.78g	23%
Sugar 51.34g	
Protein 29.59g	59%

Strawberry Whole Wheat Banana Muffins

2	eggs		2	cups whole wheat flour
1/2 cup	applesauce, unsweetened		½	cup oats
1/4 cup	vegetable oil			1 tsp baking soda
3/4 cup	packed brown sugar		1	Tbs ground cinnamon
1 tsp	vanilla extract		1	cup strawberries, frozen, sliced
3	bananas, mashed			

Procedure

1. Preheat the oven to 375°. Grease 12 large muffin cups, or line with paper liners.
2. In a large bowl, whisk together eggs, applesauce, oil, brown sugar, vanilla and bananas.
3. Combine the flour, oats, baking soda and cinnamon; Stir into the banana mixture until moistened.
4. Stir in the strawberries until evenly distributed. Spoon batter into muffin cups until completely filled.
5. Bake for 20 minutes in preheated oven, or until the tops of the muffins spring back when pressed lightly. Cool before removing from the muffin tins.

Servings: 12

Nutrition Facts

Serving size: 1/12 of a recipe (4 ounces).
Percent daily values based on the Reference Daily Intake (RDI) for a 2000 calorie diet.
Nutrition information calculated from recipe ingredients.

Amount Per Serving	
Calories	246.53
Calories From Fat (22%)	54.52
	% Daily Value
Total Fat 6.2g	**10%**
Saturated Fat 0.74g	4%
Cholesterol 35.25mg	**12%**
Sodium 123.3mg	**5%**
Potassium 260.99mg	**7%**
Total Carbohydrates 44.04g	**15%**
Fiber 2.82g	11%
Sugar 18.15g	
Protein 4.79g	**10%**

Whole Wheat Waffles

4   eggs, separated
3 Tbs   oil
2 cups   whole wheat pastry flour
1 cup   milk
2 tsp   baking powder
½ cup   sunflower seeds, optional

Procedure

1. Mix egg yolks, milk and oil together.
2. In separate bowl, stir baking powder, flour and sunflower seeds.
3. Add milk mixture to flour mixture and lightly mix.
4. Beat egg whites until stiff, but not dry. Fold whites into batter.
5. Spoon mixture onto hot waffle iron and bake until golden brown.

Servings: 7

Nutrition Facts

Serving size: 1/7 of a recipe (3.9 ounces).
Percent daily values based on the Reference Daily Intake (RDI) for a 2000 calorie diet.
Nutrition information calculated from recipe ingredients.

Amount Per Serving	
Calories	260
Calories From Fat (38%)	99.48
	% Daily Value
Total Fat 11.29g	17%
Saturated Fat 2.33g	12%
Cholesterol 123.65mg	41%
Sodium 194.59mg	8%
Potassium 151.75mg	4%
Total Carbohydrates 30.09g	10%
Fiber 1.31g	5%
Sugar 2.17g	
Protein 9.18g	18%

Entrees

Nutritious and delicious entrees for lunch or dinner. Eat dinner at least three hours before you go to bed to promote healthy digestion.

"After a good dinner one can forgive anybody,
even one's own relations."

~Oscar Wilde

Acapulco Chicken Pizza

If you like a thin crust pizza then this is for you! Also makes a great appetizer when made on small tortillas.

1	Tbs	vegetable oil
3/4 lb		fresh boneless, skinless chicken breasts, sliced
1		package Ortega® Taco Seasoning Mix
3	Tbs	cayenne pepper
5	Tbs	Ortega® Medium Taco Sauce
2		12-inch whole wheat tortillas
8	oz	Ortega® Refried Beans

1/4 cup		Ortega® Medium Taco Sauce
1/4 cup		Monterey Jack cheese, grated
1/4 cup		cheddar cheese, grated
2	cups	lettuce, shredded
2		avocados, seeded, peeled and mashed
1		tomato, diced and seeded

Procedure

1 Add oil to a large heated skillet; stir in chicken, taco seasoning mix and cayenne pepper and cook until browned. Stir in first amount of taco sauce and remove from the heat.

2 On a large plate, place flour tortillas; divide and spread with refried beans, being sure to cover the entire tortilla. Add the chicken mixture over the beans and sprinkle remaining taco sauce, grated Monterey Jack cheese, and grated cheddar cheese on top.

3 Bake in a 375° oven until the cheese is bubbly, about 10 minutes. Remove and cut into wedges. Serve with shredded lettuce, mashed avocados, and diced tomato.

Servings: 4

Total Time:

Nutrition Facts

Serving size: 1/4 of a recipe.
Percent daily values based on the Reference Daily Intake (RDI) for a 2000 calorie diet.
Nutrition information provided by the recipe author.

Amount Per Serving	
Calories	660
Calories From Fat (41%)	271.19
	% Daily Value
Total Fat 31g	48%
Saturated Fat 7g	35%
Cholesterol 0mg	0%
Sodium 1220mg	51%
Total Carbohydrates 63g	21%
Fiber 12g	48%
Protein 37g	74%

Baked Halibut with Orzo

4	Tbs	extra-virgin olive oil, divided		1		garlic clove, minced
2	Tbs	fresh lemon juice		4	cups	(packed) baby spinach
2		6- to 7-ounce halibut fillets		1	cup	halved cherry tomatoes
1	cup	orzo (rice-shaped pasta)				

Procedure

1. Preheat oven to 425°.
2. Whisk 2 tablespoons oil and lemon juice in bowl; Place halibut on rimmed baking sheet; sprinkle with salt and pepper. Drizzle oil and juice on halibut. Bake until just opaque in center, about 12 minutes.
3. Meanwhile, cook pasta in large saucepan of boiling salted water until tender but still firm to bite; drain. Add 2 tablespoons oil and garlic to same saucepan; sauté over medium heat 1 minute. Add drained pasta, spinach and tomatoes; stir to coat. Season with salt and pepper.
4. Remove from heat; cover. Let stand 1 minute (spinach will wilt). Divide pasta between 2 plates. Top with halibut and remaining dressing.

Servings: 2

Nutrition Facts

Serving size: 1/2 of a recipe
Percent daily values based on the Reference Daily Intake (RDI) for a 2000 calorie diet.
Nutrition information calculated from recipe ingredients.

Amount Per Serving	
Calories	654.14
Calories From Fat (26%)	170.54
	% Daily Value
Total Fat 19.19g	**30%**
Saturated Fat 2.59g	**13%**
Cholesterol 54.4mg	**18%**
Sodium 152.89mg	**6%**
Potassium 1433.43mg	**41%**
Total Carbohydrates 70.29g	**23%**
Fiber 4.25g	**17%**
Sugar 0.63g	
Protein 48.62g	**97%**

Balsamic Buttered Tilapia with Asparagus

This dish is best served with Thyme Potatoes.

1/4 cup	balsamic vinegar	6	4- to 5-ounce tilapia fillets
1	garlic clove, minced	1/2 cup	(1 stick) plus 1 tablespoon chilled unsalted butter, cut into 1/2-inch cubes
2	cups asparagus		
2	Tbs olive oil		salt & pepper to taste

Procedure

1. In a small sauce pan combine balsamic vinegar and garlic. Heat on medium until the sauce becomes a thick syrup. This should take about 5 minutes. Set aside.
2. Trim stem ends from asparagus. Cook asparagus in boiling salted water until crisp-tender, about 6-8 minutes. Drain. Return to same pan; set aside.
3. Heat 1 tablespoon oil in each of 2 large skillets over high heat. Sprinkle fish with salt and pepper. Sauté fish until golden, about 2 minutes per side.
4. Place balsamic vinegar syrup from step one over medium-low heat. Whisk in 1/2 cup butter 1 piece at a time. Add remaining 1 tablespoon butter to asparagus; stir over medium heat until warmed. Season with salt and pepper.
5. Divide tilapia and asparagus among plates; drizzle with sauce.

Servings: 6

Nutrition Facts

Serving size: 1/6 of a recipe (8.6 ounces).
Percent daily values based on the Reference Daily Intake (RDI) for a 2000 calorie diet.
Nutrition information calculated from recipe ingredients.

Amount Per Serving	
Calories	334.97
Calories From Fat (57%)	192
	% Daily Value
Total Fat 21.84g	**34%**
Saturated Fat 10.8g	**54%**
Cholesterol 118.91mg	**40%**
Sodium 135.45mg	**6%**
Potassium 696.33mg	**20%**
Total Carbohydrates 2.56g	**<1%**
Fiber 0.95g	**4%**
Sugar 0.86g	
Protein 31.88g	**64%**

Beefy Green Chile and Cheese Bake

Mexican style casserole topped with beef, cheese and chiles.

2	cups	crushed tortilla chips	1/2 cup	shredded cheddar cheese, divided
2	Tbs	water	1/2 cup	shredded Monterey Jack cheese, divided
1		large egg, slightly beaten	1-1/2	cups Ortega® Salsa Prima
1	lb	ground beef, cooked and drained	1/2 cup	diced green bell pepper
1		envelope dry onion soup mix		
1		(4-oz.) can Ortega® Diced Green Chiles		

Procedure

1. Preheat oven to 350°. Grease 9-inch square baking dish.
2. Combine chips, water and egg in small bowl. Press into prepared baking dish; bake for 10 minutes.
3. Combine beef, soup mix, chiles, ¼ cup cheddar cheese and ¼ cup Monterey Jack cheese in medium bowl. Spread over tortilla crust. Top with salsa, bell pepper, remaining cheddar cheese and remaining Monterey Jack cheese.
4. Bake for 25 to 30 minutes or until cheese is melted.

Servings: 4

Nutrition Facts

Serving size: 1/4 of a recipe (15.1 ounces).
Percent daily values based on the Reference Daily Intake (RDI) for a 2000 calorie diet.
Nutrition information calculated from recipe ingredients.

Amount Per Serving	
Calories	1060.94
Calories From Fat (54%)	574.73
	% Daily Value
Total Fat 64.11g	**99%**
Saturated Fat 21.25g	**106%**
Cholesterol 165.82mg	**55%**
Sodium 2336.95mg	**97%**
Potassium 984.79mg	**28%**
Total Carbohydrates 85.83g	**29%**
Fiber 10.37g	**41%**
Sugar 4.71g	
Protein 39.14g	**78%**

Black Bean with Peppers & Cumin Vinaigrette

1 1/4	cups	dried black beans, soaked	1 Tbs	chopped cilantro + extra for garnish
4	cups	water	2 Tbs	olive oil
1		bay leaf	1/2	red pepper, diced
1/2 tsp		salt	1/2	yellow pepper,
1 Tbs		red wine vinegar	1/2 cup	diced tomatoes
1		clove garlic, minced	1/2	green peppers
1/4 tsp		cumin	1	red onion, diced
1 tsp		hot pepper sauce	4	green onions, thinly sliced

Procedure

1. Drain beans & rinse well. Put in a large pot with the water & bay leaf. Bring to a boil & simmer for 1 to 1 1/2 hours. Drain and set aside.
2. Combine salt, vinegar, garlic, cumin, hot pepper sauce, cilantro and olive oil in a small bowl. Pour over warm beans and tomatoes. Toss well. Add remaining ingredients. Toss gently and garnish with fresh cilantro. Serve at room temperature.

Servings: 2

Nutrition Facts

Serving size: 1/2 of a recipe (28.1 ounces).
Percent daily values based on the Reference Daily Intake (RDI) for a 2000 calorie diet.
Nutrition information calculated from recipe ingredients.

Amount Per Serving	
Calories	318.9
Calories From Fat (40%)	127.84
	% Daily Value
Total Fat 14.55g	22%
Saturated Fat 2.05g	10%
Cholesterol 0mg	0%
Sodium 667.73mg	28%
Potassium 767.46mg	22%
Total Carbohydrates 38.81g	13%
Fiber 12.8g	51%
Sugar 3.18g	
Protein 11.97g	24%

Chicken Puttanesca

4	tsp	extra-virgin olive oil, divided	1/2 cup		kalamata olives, pitted and chopped
4		large boneless, skinless, thin-sliced chicken breast cutlets (4 ounces each)	2	Tbs	capers, drained
		Salt and black pepper	1/4 tsp		crushed red pepper flakes
6		garlic cloves, minced	1	Tbs	fresh lemon juice
1		can (28 ounces) plum tomatoes, chopped	1/4 cup		chopped fresh basil
			16	oz	whole-wheat pasta such as spaghetti

Procedure

1. Preheat oven to 250°. Warm 2 teaspoons oil in a large nonstick skillet over medium-high heat until hot. Season cutlets with salt and pepper; add to hot pan and cook 2 minutes, until browned. Flip; cook 30 seconds. Transfer cutlets to a baking sheet; cover with foil and place in oven to keep warm.

2. Add remaining 2 teaspoons of oil to the same skillet over medium heat. Add garlic and cook 10 seconds, stirring. Add tomatoes, olives, capers, and pepper flakes and bring to a simmer. Cook 5 minutes, until slightly thickened, stirring to break up tomatoes. Stir in lemon juice and basil.

3. Meanwhile, cook pasta according to package directions; drain. Toss with tomato sauce; serve with cutlets.

Servings: 4

Nutrition Facts

Serving size: 1/4 of a recipe (20.1 ounces).
Percent daily values based on the Reference Daily Intake (RDI) for a 2000 calorie diet.
Nutrition information calculated from recipe ingredients.

Amount Per Serving	
Calories	489.25
Calories From Fat (21%)	104.64
	% Daily Value
Total Fat 11.76g	18%
Saturated Fat 1.46g	7%
Cholesterol 136.88mg	46%
Sodium 1031.97mg	43%
Potassium 1150.02mg	33%
Total Carbohydrates 35.81g	12%
Fiber 5.84g	23%
Sugar 10.91g	
Protein 60.83g	122%

Chicken Sherry

Chicken Sherry goes great with garlic potatoes.

4		skinless, boneless chicken breast halves	1	cup	chicken broth
1/4 cup		all-purpose flour	3		clove garlic, minced
1	tsp	ground black pepper	1		lemon
1	Tbs	olive oil	4		carrots
1	cup	sherry (use the real stuff, not cooking sherry)	4		zucchini squashes, julienned

Procedure

1. Rinse chicken and pat dry with a paper towel. Place chicken in a resealable plastic bag with flour and pepper. Seal bag and shake to coat. Remove chicken from bag, shaking off excess flour.

2. Heat oil in a large skillet over medium high heat. Brown chicken on each side for about 5 minutes, or until golden. Remove from skillet and set aside.

3. In same skillet, combine sherry, broth, garlic and a squeeze of lemon and bring to a boil. Return chicken to skillet; reduce heat to low and simmer for 15 to 20 minutes, or until chicken is cooked through and no longer pink inside.

4. In the meantime, sauté carrots and zucchini in a separate medium skillet until they are tender. Add to simmering chicken and sauce. Heat through before serving.

Servings: 4

Nutrition Facts

Serving size: 1/4 of a recipe (27.8 ounces).
Percent daily values based on the Reference Daily Intake (RDI) for a 2000 calorie diet.
Nutrition information calculated from recipe ingredients.

Amount Per Serving	
Calories	503.3
Calories From Fat (13%)	66.77
	% Daily Value
Total Fat 7.52g	12%
Saturated Fat 1.5g	8%
Cholesterol 136.88mg	46%
Sodium 436.86mg	18%
Potassium 1853.31mg	53%
Total Carbohydrates 31.84g	11%
Fiber 6.27g	25%
Sugar 9.66g	
Protein 61.59g	123%

Chicken Wrap

4	oz	grilled chicken breast	1	leaf	lettuce
1/2 cup		non-fat refried beans	1	slice	tomatoes
4	Tbs	salsa			jalapeno pepper slices, seeded (optional)
1		whole wheat tortilla			

Procedure

1. Spread refried beans over tortilla.
2. Place chicken, salsa, lettuce, tomatoes and jalapenos on tortilla.
3. Roll up and enjoy!

Nutrition Facts

Serving size: Entire recipe (12.9 ounces).
Percent daily values based on the Reference Daily Intake (RDI) for a 2000 calorie diet.
Nutrition information calculated from recipe ingredients.

Amount Per Serving	
Calories	441.37
Calories From Fat (17%)	77.03
	% Daily Value
Total Fat 8.76g	13%
Saturated Fat 2.91g	15%
Cholesterol 106.47mg	35%
Sodium 1036.36mg	43%
Potassium 918.88mg	26%
Total Carbohydrates 43.48g	14%
Fiber 8.17g	33%
Sugar 2.97g	
Protein 46.12g	92%

Cilantro Chicken

1/4 cup	olive oil		1	15-ounce can pinto beans, drained and rinsed
8	skinless, boneless chicken breast halves		1	15-ounce can black beans, drained and rinsed
1/2 cup	all-purpose flour		1	15-ounce can whole kernel corn, drained
1	medium onion, diced			
1	red bell pepper, diced		1	4-ounce can diced green chile peppers, drained
4	cloves garlic, minced			
2 cups	chicken broth		3/4 cup	coarsely chopped fresh cilantro
2 cups	brown rice		1 tsp	salt
1	28-ounce can stewed tomatoes		1/2 tsp	pepper
			1/4 tsp	ground cayenne pepper

Procedure

1. Heat olive oil in a large skillet over medium heat. Dredge chicken in flour to coat. Place chicken in skillet and cook just until browned on all sides; set aside.

2. Stir onion, bell pepper and garlic into skillet. Cook 5 minutes, until tender. Pour in chicken broth. Mix in the brown rice, stewed tomatoes, pinto beans, black beans, corn, diced green chile peppers and cilantro. Season with salt, pepper and cayenne pepper. Bring to a boil. Return chicken to skillet. Reduce heat to low; cover and simmer 30 minutes, until rice is tender and chicken juices run clear.

Servings: 8

Nutrition Facts

Serving size: 1/8 of a recipe (22.8 ounces).
Percent daily values based on the Reference Daily Intake (RDI) for a 2000 calorie diet.
Nutrition information calculated from recipe ingredients.

Amount Per Serving	
Calories	578.8
Calories From Fat (18%)	104.31
	% Daily Value
Total Fat 11.8g	**18%**
Saturated Fat 2.12g	**11%**
Cholesterol 136.88mg	**46%**
Sodium 1260.99mg	**53%**
Potassium 1345.94mg	**38%**
Total Carbohydrates 51g	**17%**
Fiber 9.68g	**39%**
Sugar 7.63g	
Protein 66.26g	**133%**

Cinnamon Chicken with Couscous

4		whole chicken legs (about 3 pounds), cut into leg and thigh pieces	1	cup	chopped onions
		salt	3/4	cup	mixed chopped dried fruit (such as currants, apricots and prunes)
		pepper	1		14-ounce can low-salt chicken broth
2	tsp	ground cinnamon, divided	1	cup	couscous
1	tsp	ground ginger, divided	2	tsp	finely chopped fresh mint, divided
1	Tbs	olive oil			

Procedure

1. Preheat oven to 375°. Sprinkle chicken with salt, pepper, 1 teaspoon cinnamon and 1/2 teaspoon ginger. Heat oil in large ovenproof skillet over medium-high heat. Add chicken pieces, skin side down, and cook until skin is brown, about 8 minutes. Turn chicken and transfer skillet to oven. Roast chicken until thermometer inserted into thickest part of thigh registers 175°, about 15 minutes. Transfer chicken to plate; tent with foil.

2. Add onion to drippings in same skillet; sauté onion over medium-high heat until beginning to brown, about 5 minutes. Add dried fruit and remaining 1 teaspoon cinnamon and 1/2 teaspoon ginger; stir to coat. Add broth; bring to boil. Remove skillet from heat; stir in couscous and 1 teaspoon mint. Cover and let stand 5 minutes. Season couscous to taste with salt and pepper.

3. Mound couscous on platter; place chicken atop couscous. Sprinkle with 1 teaspoon mint and serve.

Servings: 4

Nutrition Facts

Serving size: 1/4 of a recipe (11.6 ounces).
Percent daily values based on the Reference Daily Intake (RDI) for a 2000 calorie diet.
Nutrition information calculated from recipe ingredients.

Percent daily values based on the Reference Daily Intake (RDI) for a 2000 calorie diet.
Nutrition information calculated from recipe ingredients.

Amount Per Serving	
Calories	458.38
Calories From Fat (15%)	67.64
	% Daily Value
Total Fat 7.59g	**12%**
Saturated Fat 1.48g	7%
Cholesterol 62.4mg	**21%**
Sodium 417.18mg	**17%**
Potassium 858.42mg	**25%**
Total Carbohydrates 74.53g	**25%**
Fiber 7.85g	31%
Sugar 1.75g	
Protein 25.21g	**50%**

Crab Quiche

1-2		Wasa™ bread (crackers)	1	Tbs	minced onion
1		egg, beaten	2	Tbs	skimmed milk
1	Tbs	bran	1/8 tsp		dry mustard
1		egg beaten		dash	pepper
1 1/2	oz	crab meat	1/8 tsp		garlic powder
1/4 cup		cooked mushrooms			
1	tsp	minced parsley			

Procedure

1. Soak Wasa™ bread crackers in beaten egg for about 15 minutes or until soft. Add 1 Tbs bran and mix. Spray 4 ½ inch pie tin with non-stick spray and press Wasa™ bread mixture into pan and up sides.
2. Beat egg, add crab, mushrooms, parsley, onion, milk and seasonings. Pour into prepared shell and bake at 375° for 25 minutes or until just set.

Servings: 1

Nutrition Facts

Serving size: Entire recipe (8.1 ounces).
Percent daily values based on the Reference Daily Intake (RDI) for a 2000 calorie diet.
Nutrition information calculated from recipe ingredients.

Amount Per Serving	
Calories	293.63
Calories From Fat (36%)	106.54
	% Daily Value
Total Fat 11.88g	**18%**
Saturated Fat 3.63g	**18%**
Cholesterol 450.52mg	**150%**
Sodium 287.97mg	**12%**
Potassium 445.64mg	**13%**
Total Carbohydrates 23.22g	**8%**
Fiber 4.37g	**17%**
Sugar 3.45g	
Protein 24.77g	**50%**

Easy Edamame

Edamame is a great snack or side dish. It is a vegetable that is high in protein and fiber. Edamame is a bean, but has a subtle nutty flavor.

How to eat: Take pod by the stem, place between teeth, strip soybeans from the pod with your teeth and discard empty pods.

2   cups edamame

dash sea salt

Procedure

1. Boil 6-8 cups of water.
2. Toss edamame in boiling water for 2 minutes.
3. Sprinkle shells with sea salt.

Nutrition Facts

Serving size: Entire recipe (5.5 ounces).
Percent daily values based on the Reference Daily Intake (RDI) for a 2000 calorie diet.
Nutrition information calculated from recipe ingredients.

Amount Per Serving	
Calories	189
Calories From Fat (35%)	66.84
	% Daily Value
Total Fat 8g	12%
Saturated Fat 1g	5%
Cholesterol 0mg	0%
Sodium 164.03mg	7%
Potassium 0.03mg	<1%
Total Carbohydrates 16g	5%
Fiber 8.1g	32%
Sugar 3g	
Protein 16.9g	34%

Easy Reuben

2	slices	whole grain or rye bread	1	tsp	mustard
4	oz	lean meat (turkey pastrami or corned beef)	1		kosher pickle (optional)
4	oz	sauerkraut			

Procedure

1. Toast bread. Warm sauerkraut and meat together in pan.
2. Spread mustard on toast.
3. Place meat and sauerkraut mixture on sandwich.

Nutrition Facts

Serving size: Entire recipe (11.5 ounces).

Percent daily values based on the Reference Daily Intake (RDI) for a 2000 calorie diet.

Nutrition information calculated from recipe ingredients.

Amount Per Serving	
Calories	335.61
Calories From Fat (20%)	65.75
	% Daily Value
Total Fat 7.4g	**11%**
Saturated Fat 1.81g	**9%**
Cholesterol 77.18mg	**26%**
Sodium 2726.01mg	**114%**
Potassium 732.95mg	**21%**
Total Carbohydrates 41.57g	**14%**
Fiber 7.18g	**29%**
Sugar 7.17g	
Protein 25.36g	**51%**

Fish Tacos

1	cup	corn	2	Tbs	cayenne pepper
1/2 cup		diced red onion	1	Tbs	ground black pepper
1	cup	peeled, chopped jicama	2	Tbs	salt
			6		4-ounce tilapia fillets
1/2 cup		diced red bell pepper	2	Tbs	olive oil
1	cup	fresh cilantro leaves, finely chopped	12		corn tortillas, warmed
1		lime, zested and juiced			
2	Tbs	sour cream			

Procedure

1 Preheat grill for high heat.

2 In a medium bowl, mix together corn, red onion, jicama, red bell pepper and cilantro. Stir in lime juice and zest.

3 In a small bowl, combine cayenne pepper, ground black pepper, and salt. Brush each fillet with olive oil and sprinkle with spices.

4 Arrange fillets on grill grate and cook for 3 minutes per side. For each fiery fish taco, top two corn tortillas with fish, sour cream and corn salsa.

Servings: 6

Nutrition Facts

Serving size: 1/6 of a recipe (11.3 ounces).
Percent daily values based on the Reference Daily Intake (RDI) for a 2000 calorie diet.
Nutrition information calculated from recipe ingredients.

Amount Per Serving	
Calories	357.51
Calories From Fat (23%)	81.06
	% Daily Value
Total Fat 9.25g	**14%**
Saturated Fat 1.8g	**9%**
Cholesterol 80.19mg	**27%**
Sodium 2548.26mg	**106%**
Potassium 897.14mg	**26%**
Total Carbohydrates 34.61g	**12%**
Fiber 6.27g	**25%**
Sugar 2.6g	
Protein 35.45g	**71%**

Fresh Broccoli and Beef Stir Fry

6	tsp	olive oil, divided
1	tsp	sugar
1/2	tsp	salt
1	tsp	ground ginger, divided
	dash	pepper
1	lb	beef flank steak, thinly sliced
2	Tbs	cornstarch

1	cup	beef broth
3	Tbs	soy sauce
1	Tbs	apple cider vinegar
1 1/2	lbs	fresh broccoli florets
1		8-ounce can sliced water chestnuts, drained
1/4	cup	chopped green onions
4	cups	hot cooked brown rice

Procedure

1. In a shallow glass container, combine 2 teaspoons of oil, sugar, salt, half of the ginger, and pepper. Add beef and turn to coat. Let stand for 15 minutes.
2. In a small bowl, combine the cornstarch, broth, soy sauce, vinegar and remaining ginger until blended; set aside.
3. In a large skillet or wok, brown beef in 2 teaspoons oil. Remove and keep warm. Add broccoli, water chestnuts and onions; stir-fry for 1 minute. Stir cornstarch mixture; add to the skillet. Bring to a boil, stirring constantly; cook and stir for 2 minutes or until thickened. Return beef to the pan; heat through. Serve over rice.

Servings: 6

Nutrition Facts

Serving size: 1/6 of a recipe (12.7 ounces).
Percent daily values based on the Reference Daily Intake (RDI) for a 2000 calorie diet.
Nutrition information calculated from recipe ingredients.

Amount Per Serving	
Calories	357.81
Calories From Fat (27%)	96.76
	% Daily Value
Total Fat 10.78g	17%
Saturated Fat 2.86g	14%
Cholesterol 22.81mg	8%
Sodium 799.22mg	33%
Potassium 713.51mg	20%
Total Carbohydrates 42.99g	14%
Fiber 3.13g	13%
Sugar 1.98g	
Protein 23.54g	47%

Fresh Fajitas

6		cloves garlic	
1/2		red onion, chopped	
2		limes, juiced	
1		medium jalapeno chile pepper	
2	Tbs	fresh thyme leaves	
1	cup	loosely packed cilantro leaves	
3/4 cup		olive oil	
2	Tbs	honey	
3	lbs	beef flank steak	

1 red onion, sliced into thin strips
1 green bell pepper, sliced into thin strips
1 red bell pepper, sliced into thin strips
1 sweet yellow pepper, sliced into thin strips
2 garlic cloves, minced
   flour tortillas

Procedure

1. Puree garlic, onion, lime juice, jalapeño, thyme, cilantro, olive oil and honey with a blender or food processor until ingredients are well blended.

2. Place the flank steak with ¼ cup of the mixture in a resealable bag. Place the onions, peppers and minced garlic in ¼ cup of the mixture in a separate resealable bag. Marinate both overnight in refrigerator. Reserve the rest of the puree to use later as a sauce.

3. Preheat grill for medium-high heat. While grill is warming, remove the meat and veggies from the refrigerator and let sit at room temperature for at least 30 minutes. Discard any marinade left in the bag. Liberally season the steak with the kosher salt and cook to desired doneness, approximately 4 minutes per side for medium-rare.Add the vegetables to grill. Grill until desired doneness, about 7 minutes, stirring occasionally.

4. Warm the tortillas on the grill. Slice the steak against the grain into 1/8 to 1/4 inch slices and drizzle the remaining marinade over the meat and vegetables. Serve!

Nutrition Facts

Serving size: 1/10 of a recipe (9.3 ounces).
Percent daily values based on the Reference Daily Intake (RDI) for a 2000 calorie diet.
Nutrition information calculated from recipe ingredients.

Amount Per Serving	
Calories	478.68
Calories From Fat (51%)	244.27
	% Daily Value
Total Fat 27.17g	42%
Saturated Fat 6.26g	31%
Cholesterol 40.82mg	14%
Sodium 282.59mg	12%
Potassium 642.27mg	18%
Total Carbohydrates 26.19g	9%
Fiber 2.71g	11%
Sugar 5.23g	
Protein 32.5g	65%

Greek Pasta with Chicken

1	lb	uncooked whole wheat penne pasta	3		roma tomatoes
2	Tbs	olive oil	1/2 cup		crumbled feta cheese
3		cloves garlic, crushed	3	Tbs	chopped fresh parsley
1/2 cup		chopped red onion	2	Tbs	lemon juice
1	lb	skinless, boneless chicken breast meat, cut into bite-size pieces	2	tsp	dried oregano
1		14-ounce can marinated artichoke hearts, drained and chopped			salt and pepper to taste

Procedure

1. Bring a large pot of lightly salted water to a boil. Cook pasta according to directions until al dente . Drain and set aside.
2. Meanwhile, heat olive oil in a large skillet over medium-high heat. Add garlic and onion and sauté for 2 minutes. Stir in the chicken. Cook, stirring occasionally, until chicken is no longer pink and the juices run clear, about 5 to 6 minutes.
3. Reduce heat to medium-low. Add the artichoke hearts, tomato, feta cheese, parsley, lemon juice, oregano and cooked pasta. Stir until heated through, about 2 to 3 minutes. Remove from heat; season to taste with salt and pepper.

Servings: 6

Nutrition Facts

Serving size: 1/6 of a recipe (8.6 ounces).
Percent daily values based on the Reference Daily Intake (RDI) for a 2000 calorie diet.
Nutrition information calculated from recipe ingredients.

Amount Per Serving	
Calories	428.58
Calories From Fat (18%)	77.16
	% Daily Value
Total Fat 8.97g	14%
Saturated Fat 2.53g	13%
Cholesterol 17.99mg	6%
Sodium 226.69mg	9%
Potassium 303.33mg	9%
Total Carbohydrates 71.54g	24%
Fiber 8.27g	33%
Sugar 3.63g	
Protein 18.1g	36%

Grilled Cherry Pork Chops

3	Tbs	balsamic vinegar		1	lb	sour cherries (about 3 cups), pitted
3	Tbs	sugar		1	Tbs	cornstarch dissolved in 1 tablespoon cold water
3/4 cup		dry red wine				
1/4 cup		minced shallots		2	tsp	fresh lime juice, or to taste
1		3-inch cinnamon stick		8		1-inch-thick boneless pork chops
1	cup	chicken broth				vegetable oil
						salt and pepper

Procedure

1. In a heavy saucepan, boil vinegar and sugar over moderate heat until the mixture is reduced to a glaze. Add wine, shallot the cinnamon stick and boil the mixture until it is reduced to about 1/4 cup. Add the broth and the cherries and simmer the sauce for 5 minutes. Stir the cornstarch mixture. Add enough of it to the sauce, stirring, to thicken the sauce to the desired consistency, and simmer the sauce for 2 minutes. Discard the cinnamon stick. Stir in the lime juice and salt and pepper to taste, keeping the sauce warm and covered.

2. Pat the chops dry with paper towels. Rub both sides of each chop with oil and season with salt and pepper. Grill the chops on an oiled rack set 5 to 6 inches over glowing coals for 6 to 8 minutes on each side, or until just cooked through. Transfer the pork chops to a platter and spoon the sauce over them.

Servings: 8

Nutrition Facts

Serving size: 1/8 of a recipe (8.1 ounces).
Percent daily values based on the Reference Daily Intake (RDI) for a 2000 calorie diet.
Nutrition information calculated from recipe ingredients.

Amount Per Serving	
Calories	238.17
Calories From Fat (30%)	70.31
	% Daily Value
Total Fat 7.93g	12%
Saturated Fat 1.16g	6%
Cholesterol 51.15mg	17%
Sodium 269.95mg	11%
Potassium 605.84mg	17%
Total Carbohydrates 16.52g	6%
Fiber 2.85g	11%
Sugar 9.93g	
Protein 22.29g	45%

Italian Sausage and Polenta

1	lb	sweet Italian turkey sausage, cut into 1/2" pieces	4	cups	hot cooked creamy polenta*
1		medium red pepper, cut into 1" strips	4	cups	water
2		fennel bulbs, cut into wedges	1	tsp	salt
6		roma tomatoes, cut into wedges	1	cups	polenta (not quick-cooking) or yellow cornmeal (10 oz)
2	tsp	dried oregano leaves, crushed			Parmesan cheese, grated (optional)
1 1/2		cups chicken broth			

Procedure

1. Preheat oven to 425°. Spray roasting pan with vegetable cooking spray.
2. Mix sausage, pepper, fennel, tomatoes, oregano and 1/2 cup broth in pan.
3. Roast 30 minutes or until done, stirring once.
4. Stir in remaining broth. Serve with pan juices over polenta (see directions below). Garnish with freshly grated Parmesan cheese, if desired.
5. *To cook polenta, bring water and salt to a boil in a 4-quart heavy pot, then add polenta in a thin stream, whisking. Cook over medium heat, whisking for 2 minutes. Reduce heat to low and simmer polenta, covered, stirring for 1 minute after every 10 minutes of cooking, 45 minutes total. Remove from heat and serve warm.

Servings: 6

Nutrition Facts

Serving size: 1/6 of a recipe (16.5 ounces).
Percent daily values based on the Reference Daily Intake (RDI) for a 2000 calorie diet.
Nutrition information calculated from recipe ingredients.

Amount Per Serving	
Calories	347.01
Calories From Fat (45%)	157.36
	% Daily Value
Total Fat 18.62g	**29%**
Saturated Fat 4.2g	**21%**
Cholesterol 60.4mg	**20%**
Sodium 1446.61mg	**60%**
Potassium 261.03mg	**7%**
Total Carbohydrates 34.18g	**11%**
Fiber 6.09g	**24%**
Sugar 6.74g	
Protein 18.1g	**36%**

Maple Salmon

1	lb	salmon	1		clove garlic, minced
1/4	cup	maple syrup	1/4	tsp	garlic salt
2	Tbs	soy sauce	1/8	tsp	ground black pepper

Procedure

1. In a small bowl, mix the maple syrup, soy sauce, garlic, garlic salt and pepper.
2. Place salmon in a shallow glass baking dish and coat with the maple syrup mixture. Cover the dish and marinate salmon in the refrigerator 30 minutes, turning once. (DO NOT marinate for more than 30 minutes.)
3. Preheat oven to 400°. Place the baking dish in preheated oven and bake salmon uncovered 20 minutes, or until easily flaked with a fork.

Servings: 4

Nutrition Facts

Serving size: 1/4 of a recipe (5.1 ounces).
Percent daily values based on the Reference Daily Intake (RDI) for a 2000 calorie diet.
Nutrition information calculated from recipe ingredients.

Amount Per Serving	
Calories	267.49
Calories From Fat (29%)	76.96
	% Daily Value
Total Fat 8.56g	13%
Saturated Fat 1.82g	9%
Cholesterol 64.64mg	22%
Sodium 490.16mg	20%
Potassium 577.06mg	16%
Total Carbohydrates 14.62g	5%
Fiber 0.17g	<1%
Sugar 12.14g	
Protein 31.55g	63%

Orange Chicken

6	chicken breasts, boned and skinned	8	oz	frozen concentrate orange juice
1/2 tsp	ginger	1 1/2		cups shredded coconut
1 tsp	salt	2	cups	orange segments or canned mandarin oranges
	pepper	2		green onions, chopped

Procedure

1. Put chicken, ginger, salt, pepper and frozen orange juice in crock pot and cook on low 6 hours. Serve chicken with hot cooked brown rice on platter.
2. Top with coconut, orange segments and green onions. Serve chicken liquid in gravy boat, if desired.

Serve with brown rice and steamed broccoli.

Servings: 6

Nutrition Facts

Serving size: 1/6 of a recipe (15.1 ounces).
Percent daily values based on the Reference Daily Intake (RDI) for a 2000 calorie diet.
Nutrition information calculated from recipe ingredients.

Amount Per Serving	
Calories	742.02
Calories From Fat (45%)	333.78
	% Daily Value
Total Fat 39.66g	**61%**
Saturated Fat 33.24g	**166%**
Cholesterol 136.88mg	**46%**
Sodium 568.42mg	**24%**
Potassium 1355.78mg	**39%**
Total Carbohydrates 39.92g	**13%**
Fiber 10.36g	**41%**
Sugar 29.34g	
Protein 60.15g	**120%**

Orange Roughy Parmesan

4	6 oz	orange roughy fillets	1	cup	dry bread crumbs
2		eggs	1/3 cup		grated Parmesan cheese
1/4 cup		milk			salt and pepper to taste

Procedure

1. Preheat oven to 425°. In a shallow bowl, beat egg and milk. In another shallow bowl, combine the bread crumbs and Parmesan cheese.
2. Dip fillets in egg mixture, then coat with crumb mixture. Place in a greased 13x9 baking dish. Bake, uncovered, for 15-20 minutes or until fish flakes easily with a fork. Salt and pepper to taste.

Serve with asparagus grilled in olive oil and garlic salt.

Servings: 4

Nutrition Facts

Serving size: 1/4 of a recipe (8.8 ounces).
Percent daily values based on the Reference Daily Intake (RDI) for a 2000 calorie diet.
Nutrition information calculated from recipe ingredients.

Amount Per Serving	
Calories	344.09
Calories From Fat (22%)	76.03
	% Daily Value
Total Fat 8.53g	13%
Saturated Fat 2.89g	14%
Cholesterol 175.42mg	58%
Sodium 548.24mg	23%
Potassium 779.57mg	22%
Total Carbohydrates 20.71g	7%
Fiber 1.22g	5%
Sugar 2.74g	
Protein 43g	86%

Pita Pockets with Chickpeas and Vegetables

2		cloves garlic, minced	dash	salt (optional)
1/2 cup		scallions (green and white parts), finely chopped	dash	hot pepper sauce (optional)
2	tsp	vegetable oil	2	whole-wheat pita rounds, cut in half
1/3 cup		green bell pepper, chopped	2	small tomatoes, cut into 4 slices each and seeded
3	Tbs	fresh parsley, chopped	1	small onion, sliced
½	tsp	dried oregano	4	leaves romaine or other lettuce
½	tsp	dried mint	1 cup	alfalfa or other sprouts or lettuce
1		15-ounce can chickpeas, rinsed	1 cup	Monterey Jack or soy cheese, shredded (optional)

Procedure

1. In a skillet cook the garlic and scallions, stirring in the oil over medium heat until the scallions are soft.
2. Add the bell pepper, parsley and sesame seeds. Cook until the pepper is soft. Add the oregano and mint and cook, stirring, one minute more.
3. Place the vegetable mixture and chickpeas in a food processor and process until smooth. Add the salt and hot pepper sauce.
4. Stuff the mixture into pita pockets. Garnish with the tomatoes, onion, lettuce, sprouts and cheese.

Servings: 4

Nutrition Facts

Serving size: 1/4 of a recipe (32.8 ounces).
Percent daily values based on the Reference Daily Intake (RDI) for a 2000 calorie diet.
Nutrition information calculated from recipe ingredients.

Amount Per Serving	
Calories	481.2
Calories From Fat (27%)	130.29
	% Daily Value
Total Fat 15.04g	23%
Saturated Fat 6.11g	31%
Cholesterol 25.14mg	8%
Sodium 738.15mg	31%
Potassium 2099.41mg	60%
Total Carbohydrates 70.81g	24%
Fiber 22.4g	90%
Sugar 11.59g	
Protein 24.77g	50%

Pork Chops with Apples and Sweet Potatoes

4		pork chops	3	Tbs	brown sugar
2		onions, sliced into rings	1/2	tsp	freshly ground bla pepper
2		sweet potatoes, thinly sliced	1	tsp	salt
2		apples, peeled, cored and sliced into 1/4" rings			

Procedure

1. Preheat oven to 375°.
2. Season pork chops with salt and pepper to taste, and arrange in a medium oven-safe skillet. Top pork chops with onions, sweet potatoes and apples. Sprinkle with brown sugar. Season with 1/2 teaspoons pepper and 1 teaspoon salt.
3. Cover and bake 1 hour, until sweet potatoes are tender and pork chops have reached an internal temperature of 160°.

Servings: 4

Nutrition Facts

Serving size: 1/4 of a recipe (11.8 ounces).
Percent daily values based on the Reference Daily Intake (RDI) for a 2000 calorie diet.
Nutrition information calculated from recipe ingredients.

Amount Per Serving	
Calories	327.91
Calories From Fat (7%)	22.26
	% Daily Value
Total Fat 2.48g	4%
Saturated Fat 0.73g	4%
Cholesterol 51.15mg	17%
Sodium 768.15mg	32%
Potassium 1459.64mg	42%
Total Carbohydrates 53.8g	18%
Fiber 6.68g	27%
Sugar 20.21g	
Protein 23.15g	46%

Pork Gyros

Pork

1/4 cup	extra-virgin olive oil
1/4 cup	dry red wine
3	garlic cloves, minced
1	small bay leaf, crumbled
1/2 Tbs	(packed) fresh oregano leaves
1/2 tsp	salt
1/4 tsp	freshly ground black pepper
2	1-pound pork tenderloins

Sauce

1 1/2	cups plain Greek yogurt
2	Tbs	chopped seeded tomatoes
2	Tbs	chopped fresh dill
2	Tbs	drained capers, chopped
2		garlic cloves, minced
1	Tbs	tomato paste
1	Tbs	red wine vinegar
6		7-inch-diameter pita breads
1		red onion, halved, thinly sliced
2		diced roma tomatoes
24		large arugula leaves

Procedure

1. Combine extra-virgin olive oil, dry red wine, minced garlic cloves, crumbled bay leaf, fresh oregano leaves, salt and ground black pepper in a large resealable plastic bag. Shake well to blend ingredients. Add pork to the bag. Refrigerate overnight, turning bag occasionally.

2. Combine sauce ingredients—Greek yogurt, chopped seeded tomato, chopped fresh dill, chopped and drained capers, garlic cloves, tomato paste and red wine vinegar—in a medium bowl. Cover and chill until ready to use. Can be chilled up to 1 day.

3. Prepare grill (medium heat). Remove pork from bag. Grill until thermometer inserted into center of each tenderloin registers 145°, about 18 minutes. Transfer to work surface; let stand 10 minutes (temperature will rise 5 to 10 degrees). Thinly slice into rounds.

4. Grill pitas until warmed through and softened, about 2 minutes per side. Cut pitas in half. Fill pita halves with pork, drizzle with sauce, then tuck in onion, diced tomatoes and arugula. Serve, passing remaining sauce separately.   Servings: 6

Nutrition Facts

Serving size: 1/6 of a recipe (8.3 ounces).
Percent daily values based on the Reference Daily Intake (RDI) for a 2000 calorie diet.
Nutrition information calculated from recipe ingredients.

Amount Per Serving	
Calories	383.15
Calories From Fat (34%)	128.45
	% Daily Value
Total Fat 14.86g	**23%**
Saturated Fat 2.86g	**14%**
Cholesterol 27.55mg	**9%**
Sodium 715.87mg	**30%**
Potassium 495.5mg	**14%**
Total Carbohydrates 47.3g	**16%**
Fiber 6.64g	**27%**
Sugar 3.12g	
Protein 18.99g	**38%**

Roast Pork with Green Apples

2		(3/4 lb. each) whole pork tenderloins		2	Tbs	packed brown sugar
1	tsp	olive oil		1/2	tsp	ground cinnamon
1/4	tsp	coarsely ground black pepper		1-3/4		cups chicken broth
3		large Granny Smith apples, cored and thickly sliced		2	tsp	all-purpose flour
1		(1 1/2 lb.) butternut squash, peeled and cubed				

Procedure

1. Preheat oven to 425°. Spray large roasting pan with cooking spray.
2. Brush pork with oil and season with black pepper. Place in prepared pan. Mix apples, squash, brown sugar, cinnamon and 1/2 cup broth. Add to pan.
3. Roast 25 minutes or until temperature reads 155° on meat thermometer, stirring squash mixture once during roasting. Remove pork and set aside. Roast squash mixture 15 minutes or until browned. Remove squash mixture from pan.
4. Mix remaining broth and flour. Stir into pan drippings, scraping up browned bits. Cook until mixture boils and thickens, stirring constantly. Serve sauce with sliced pork and squash mixture.

Servings: 8

Nutrition Facts

Serving size: 1/8 of a recipe (8.7 ounces).
Percent daily values based on the Reference Daily Intake (RDI) for a 2000 calorie diet.
Nutrition information calculated from recipe ingredients.

Amount Per Serving	
Calories	247.5
Calories From Fat (29%)	71.33
	% Daily Value
Total Fat 7.9g	12%
Saturated Fat 2.68g	13%
Cholesterol 79.9mg	27%
Sodium 225.35mg	9%
Potassium 637.61mg	18%
Total Carbohydrates 16.72g	6%
Fiber 1.36g	5%
Sugar 9.7g	
Protein 27.12g	54%

Roasted Halibut

2	cups	loosely packed cilantro leaves (from 1 large bunch)
2	Tbs	fresh lemon juice
1		green onion, chopped (about 1/4 cup)
1	Tbs	minced peeled fresh ginger
1/2		jalapeño chile with seeds, chopped (about 2 teaspoons)
5	Tbs	safflower oil, divided
2	tsp	Asian sesame oil, divided
3	tsp	soy sauce, divided
2		8-ounce halibut fillets, each about 1-inch thick
2	cups	green beans, halved
2	cups	stemmed shiitake or oyster mushrooms

Procedure

1. Preheat oven to 450°. Place first 5 ingredients, 3 tablespoons safflower oil, 1 teaspoon sesame oil and 1 teaspoon soy sauce in processor; puree. Season sauce to taste with salt.

2. Place fish, beans and mushrooms in single layer on rimmed baking sheet. Whisk remaining 2 tablespoons safflower oil, 1 teaspoon sesame oil and 2 teaspoons soy sauce in bowl to blend. Pour over fish, beans and mushrooms; toss beans and mushrooms to coat. Sprinkle with salt and pepper. Roast until fish is opaque in center and beans are crisp-tender, about 8 minutes. Divide fish, vegetables and sauce between plates.

Servings: 2

Nutrition Facts

Serving size: 1/2 of a recipe (27.7 ounces).
Percent daily values based on the Reference Daily Intake (RDI) for a 2000 calorie diet.
Nutrition information calculated from recipe ingredients.

Amount Per Serving	
Calories	928.01
Calories From Fat (46%)	430.89
	% Daily Value
Total Fat 48.58g	75%
Saturated Fat 4.2g	21%
Cholesterol 130.56mg	44%
Sodium 524.36mg	22%
Potassium 2544.91mg	73%
Total Carbohydrates 33.86g	11%
Fiber 8.56g	34%
Sugar 8.31g	
Protein 90.81g	182%

Roasted Pepper Pork and Potatoes

4		boneless pork chops, 1/2" thick	1		medium onion, sliced
		ground black pepper	1	tsp	dried oregano leaves, crushed
1	Tbs	olive oil	1	cup	chicken broth
4		medium red potatoes, cut up	1/2 cup		diced roasted red peppers

Procedure

1. Sprinkle chops with black pepper.
2. Heat oil in nonstick skillet. Add chops and cook until well browned, about five minutes for each side. Remove chops.
3. Add potatoes, onion and oregano. Cook 5 min. or until browned, stirring occasionally.
4. Add chops, broth and peppers. Heat to a boil. Cover and cook over low heat 10 minutes or until done.

Servings: 4

Nutrition Facts

Serving size: 1/4 of a recipe (11.4 ounces).
Percent daily values based on the Reference Daily Intake (RDI) for a 2000 calorie diet.
Nutrition information calculated from recipe ingredients.

Amount Per Serving	
Calories	262.05
Calories From Fat (21%)	54.18
	% Daily Value
Total Fat 6.06g	9%
Saturated Fat 1.25g	6%
Cholesterol 51.15mg	17%
Sodium 370.58mg	15%
Potassium 1229.48mg	35%
Total Carbohydrates 26.31g	9%
Fiber 2.83g	11%
Sugar 1.32g	
Protein 25.02g	50%

Salmon with Sweet Potatoes

3		medium sweet potatoes, peeled and thinly sliced
1		medium yellow onion, roughly chopped
1	tsp	grated ginger root
1	cup	orange juice
3	Tbs	orange marmalade, divided
2	Tbs	margarine

		salt, to taste
1 1/4	lbs	salmon fillet, skin removed, cut into pieces
		freshly ground black pepper, to taste
1/4 cup		almond slivers, toasted
1/4 cup		Italian parsley sprigs

Procedure

1. Preheat oven to 400º.
2. Combine sweet potatoes, onion, ginger, juice, 2 Tbs. marmalade, margarine and salt. Place in a 9x13 casserole dish sprayed with cooking spray.
3. Bake, covered, for 40 minutes. Remove from oven; top with salmon. Brush fish with reserved 1 Tbs marmalade; grind on pepper.
4. Return to oven uncovered and bake 10 to 12 minutes, until fish is done to your liking. Garnish with almonds and parsley.

Servings: 6

Nutrition Facts

Serving size: 1/6 of a recipe (10 ounces).
Percent daily values based on the Reference Daily Intake (RDI) for a 2000 calorie diet.
Nutrition information calculated from recipe ingredients.

Amount Per Serving	
Calories	461.45
Calories From Fat (26%)	119.17
	% Daily Value
Total Fat 13.51g	21%
Saturated Fat 4.17g	21%
Cholesterol 64.04mg	21%
Sodium 94.57mg	4%
Potassium 1647.39mg	47%
Total Carbohydrates 55.76g	19%
Fiber 5.46g	22%
Sugar 25.31g	
Protein 29.81g	60%

Sausage Primavera

The whole family will love this one. It's a great way to sneak vegetables in. The first time I made this, I mulled over the the hot Italian turkey sausage because of the spiciness. There is no need for worry; everyone will love it and the turkey sausage isn't quite as hot as traditional hot Italian sausage. However, if you like spicy and want an extra kick, add more red pepper flakes.

1	16 oz	package uncooked whole wheat farfalle pasta
1	lb	hot Italian turkey sausage, cut into 1/2 inch slices
1/4 cup		olive oil
4		cloves garlic, minced
1/2		onion, diced
1		small zucchini, chopped
1		small yellow squash, chopped

9		roma (plum) tomatoes, chopped
1		green bell pepper, chopped
20		leaves fresh basil (fresh is important in this recipe)
2	cubes	chicken bouillon granules
1/2 tsp		red pepper flakes
1/2 cup		grated Parmesan cheese (you may need more if you love it like I do)

Procedure

1 Bring a large pot of lightly salted water to a boil. Place farfalle in pot and cook 8 to 10 minutes, until al dente; drain.

2 While the pasta is cooking, place sausage in a large skillet over medium heat and cook until evenly brown; set aside. Heat 1/4 cup oil in skillet. Stir in garlic and onion, and cook until tender. Mix in zucchini, squash, tomatoes, bell pepper and basil. Dissolve bouillon in the mixture. Season with red pepper. Continue cooking 10 minutes.

3 Mix pasta, sausage and cheese into skillet. Continue cooking 5 minutes, or until heated through.

Servings: 8

Nutrition Facts

Serving size: 1/8 of a recipe (10.6 ounces).
Percent daily values based on the Reference Daily Intake (RDI) for a 2000 calorie diet.
Nutrition information calculated from recipe ingredients.

Amount Per Serving	
Calories	368.32
Calories From Fat (55%)	203.88

	% Daily Value
Total Fat 23.92g	37%
Saturated Fat 5.33g	27%
Cholesterol 51.72mg	17%
Sodium 1835.22mg	76%
Potassium 324.1mg	9%
Total Carbohydrates 29.03g	10%
Fiber 5.42g	22%
Sugar 8.12g	
Protein 18.33g	37%

Shrimp Stir Fry

Omit cashews if you are sensitive. Substitute chicken for shrimp to change this one up.

1/4 cup	cornstarch
2	egg whites
1/4 tsp	salt
1 lb	uncooked large shrimp, peeled, deveined
3 Tbs	peanut oil
1 1/2 Tbs	chopped garlic
1 1/2 Tbs	chopped peeled fresh ginger

1 1/2	bunches broccoli, cut into florets
2	carrots, thinly sliced on diagonal
1/4 cup	cashews
1/4 cup	bottled teriyaki sauce
3 Tbs	dry sherry (use the real stuff, not cooking sherry)
1/4 tsp	(or more) dried crushed red pepper
1 1/2 cups	long-grain brown rice, cooked

Procedure

1. Whisk cornstarch, egg whites and salt in large bowl until smooth. Add shrimp; toss to coat. Let shrimp stand at room temperature 20 minutes.
2. Heat 2 tablespoons peanut oil in large wok or heavy large skillet over medium-high heat. Add shrimp, garlic and ginger and stir-fry until shrimp is cooked through, about 2 minutes.
3. Using slotted spoon, transfer shrimp to plate. Add remaining 1 tablespoon peanut oil to wok. Add broccoli and carrots. Stir-fry until vegetables are crisp-tender, about 4 minutes.
4. Add cashews, teriyaki sauce, sherry and 1/4 teaspoon crushed red pepper and cook 1 minute. Return shrimp to wok and stir-fry until coated with sauce and heated through, about 1 minute. Season with salt and additional crushed red pepper, if desired.
5. Spoon shrimp and vegetable mixture onto platter. Spoon cooked rice around edge of platter and serve.

Servings: 4

Nutrition Facts

Serving size: 1/4 of a recipe (11.7 ounces).
Percent daily values based on the Reference Daily Intake (RDI) for a 2000 calorie diet.
Nutrition information calculated from recipe ingredients.

Amount Per Serving	
Calories	428.08
Calories From Fat (33%)	139.77
	% Daily Value
Total Fat 15.96g	25%
Saturated Fat 2.78g	14%
Cholesterol 172.37mg	57%
Sodium 1072.71mg	45%
Potassium 603.64mg	17%
Total Carbohydrates 37.73g	13%
Fiber 2.9g	12%
Sugar 4.43g	
Protein 30.47g	61%

Stuffed Chiles in Ranch Sauce

Chiles Rellenos, stuffed chiles, are zesty and flavorful when prepared with Ranch Sauce. Filled with luscious cheese and coated in a rich beaten egg mixture.

1	Tbs	vegetable oil	2		bay leaves
1		small onion, peeled and chopped	1		cinnamon stick, broken into pieces
1		small red, green or yellow bell pepper, seeded and chopped	1/2 tsp		crushed dried oregano
			2		7-ounce cans Whole Green Chiles
1		clove garlic, peeled and finely chopped	8	oz	Monterey Jack cheese, cut into 1x2-inch strips
1		24-ounce jar Chunky Salsa	3		eggs, separated
1/2 cup		water	3	Tbs	all-purpose flour
1		Maggi® Chicken Bouillon Cube			

Procedure

For Ranch Sauce

1. Heat vegetable oil in large saucepan over medium-high heat. Add onion, bell pepper and garlic; cook, stirring constantly, for 1 to 2 minutes or until onion is tender. Stir in salsa, water, bouillon, bay leaves, cinnamon and oregano. Bring to a boil. Reduce heat to low; cook for 10 to 15 minutes or until flavors are blended. Remove bay leaves and cinnamon stick pieces.

For Stuffed Chiles

2. Stuff each chile (being careful not to break skins) with cheese. Beat egg whites in small mixer bowl until stiff peaks form. Whisk egg yolks in small bowl until creamy. Fold egg yolks and flour into egg whites until just combined.

3. Add vegetable oil to 1-inch depth in medium skillet; heat over high heat for 3 to 4 minutes. Dip chiles in batter until well coated. Place in oil; fry, turning frequently with tongs, until golden brown. Remove from skillet; place on paper towels to drain. Serve with Ranch Sauce.

Nutrition Facts

Serving size: 1/5 of a recipe.
Percent daily values based on the Reference Daily Intake (RDI) for a 2000 calorie diet.
Nutrition information calculated from recipe ingredients.

Amount Per Serving	
Calories	335.01
Calories From Fat (53%)	178.73
	% Daily Value
Total Fat 20.3g	31%
Saturated Fat 9.91g	50%
Cholesterol 167.32mg	56%
Sodium 1609.33mg	67%
Potassium 700.85mg	20%
Total Carbohydrates 22.74g	8%
Fiber 6.3g	25%
Sugar 6.46g	
Protein 18.97g	38%

Sweet Potato Burrito with Mango Salsa

Serve on a bed of lettuce. Everyone loves these burritos, even the carnivores in our family!

1	Tbs	vegetable oil		4	tsp	prepared mustard
1		onion, chopped		1	pinch	cayenne pepper, or to taste
4		cloves garlic, minced		3	Tbs	soy sauce
3	cans	black beans		4	cups	cooked and mashed sweet potatoes
2	cups	water		12		10-inch flour tortillas, warmed
3	Tbs	chili powder		8	oz	shredded cheddar cheese
2	tsp	ground cumin		1	cup	mango salsa

Procedure

1. Preheat oven to 350°.
2. Heat oil in a medium skillet, and sauté onion and garlic until soft. Turn heat to low. Stir in beans and water. Heat until warm. Remove from heat, and stir in the chili powder, cumin, mustard, cayenne pepper and soy sauce.
3. Divide bean mixture and mashed sweet potatoes evenly between the warm flour tortillas. Top with cheese. Fold tortillas burrito style, and place on a baking sheet.
4. Bake for 12 minutes in preheated oven; top with mango salsa and serve.

Servings: 12

Nutrition Facts

Serving size: 1/12 of a recipe (9.3 ounces).
Percent daily values based on the Reference Daily Intake (RDI) for a 2000 calorie diet.
Nutrition information calculated from recipe ingredients.

Amount Per Serving	
Calories	394.7
Calories From Fat (25%)	96.84
	% Daily Value
Total Fat 11.05g	17%
Saturated Fat 4.9g	25%
Cholesterol 19.85mg	7%
Sodium 779.65mg	32%
Potassium 815.26mg	23%
Total Carbohydrates 57.18g	19%
Fiber 12.83g	51%
Sugar 1.65g	
Protein 18.1g	36%

Tasty Tuna Sandwich

3	oz	tuna (packed in water)	1		egg, hardboiled and chopped
1	tsp	olive oil	2	slices	whole grain bread
1	tsp	capers, drained	1	leaf	lettuce
1	stalk	celery, sliced	1	tsp	mustard
1	Tbs	chopped red onion			

Procedure

1 Drain tuna and combine with oil, capers, red onion, celery and egg.

2 Spread mustard on bread. Add tuna mixture and lettuce.

Nutrition Facts

Serving size: Entire recipe (9.6 ounces).
Percent daily values based on the Reference Daily Intake (RDI) for a 2000 calorie diet.
Nutrition information calculated from recipe ingredients.

Amount Per Serving	
Calories	371.77
Calories From Fat (32%)	119.98

	% Daily Value
Total Fat 13.5g	**21%**
Saturated Fat 3.12g	**16%**
Cholesterol 266.67mg	**89%**
Sodium 791.4mg	**33%**
Potassium 524.45mg	**15%**
Total Carbohydrates 27.68g	**9%**
Fiber 4.59g	**18%**
Sugar 6.92g	
Protein 34.87g	**70%**

Thai Beef Salad

½	cup	fresh lime juice	10	cups	Napa cabbages, sliced very thinly
½	cup	fresh orange juice	2	cups	carrots, shredded
4	Tbs	fish sauce (usually found in Asian food section)	1	cups	fresh chopped cilantro, loosely packed
2	Tbs	rice wine vinegar	1½	lbs	flank steak
2	Tbs	dark brown sugar			kosher salt
1	Tbs	grated jalapeño (optional, and use as much as you like)			cracked black pepper
5		green onions (mostly white, with some of the green)			

Procedure

1. Preheat broiler to high. In a small bowl, whisk together lime and orange juices, fish sauce, rice wine vinegar, sugar and jalapeño. Add green onions and set aside. In a large salad bowl, toss together cabbage, carrots, mint and cilantro. Set aside.

2. Season steak with salt and pepper and place on broiler pan. Broil, turning once, until done to your liking (about 6-7 minutes per side for medium rare, 8 minutes for medium, 9-10 minutes for well). Remove meat to a cutting board and let cool 10 minutes before slicing thinly. Add to cabbage salad, then add dressing and toss to coat evenly. Serve immediately.

Servings: 4

Nutrition Facts

Serving size: 1/4 of a recipe (19.1 ounces).
Percent daily values based on the Reference Daily Intake (RDI) for a 2000 calorie diet.
Nutrition information calculated from recipe ingredients.

Amount Per Serving	
Calories	427.03
Calories From Fat (23%)	98.14
	% Daily Value
Total Fat 10.84g	17%
Saturated Fat 4.34g	22%
Cholesterol 51.03mg	17%
Sodium 1594.51mg	66%
Potassium 1682.17mg	48%
Total Carbohydrates 45.48g	15%
Fiber 8.5g	34%
Sugar 27.78g	
Protein 42.69g	85%

White Chicken Chili

1	lb	dry white beans	1 1/2	tsp	oregano
6	cups	chicken broth	1	tsp	cloves
2		garlic cloves, crushed	1/4	tsp	cayenne pepper
1 1/2		onion, chopped	4	cups	chopped cooked chicken
8	oz	green chili peppers, chopped	3	cups	chicken broth
2	tsp	cumin			

Procedure

1. In a large kettle combine dry white beans, chicken broth, crushed garlic cloves, and 1 chopped onion. Bring to a boil, reduce the heat, and simmer, covered, until the beans are tender, about 2 to 3 hours.

2. In a large skillet, sauté 1 cup chopped onions until tender. Add chopped green chili peppers, cumin, oregano, cloves and cayenne pepper; mix thoroughly. Add cooked, chopped chicken and chicken broth. Simmer for 1 hour.

Servings: 8

Nutrition Facts

Serving size: 1/8 of a recipe.
Percent daily values based on the Reference Daily Intake (RDI) for a 2000 calorie diet.
Nutrition information calculated from recipe ingredients.

Amount Per Serving	
Calories	251.12
Calories From Fat (11%)	27.33
	% Daily Value
Total Fat 2.96g	5%
Saturated Fat 0.78g	4%
Cholesterol 0mg	0%
Sodium 1363.22mg	57%
Potassium 1328.03mg	38%
Total Carbohydrates 36.39g	12%
Fiber 8.78g	35%
Sugar 2.16g	
Protein 20.28g	41%

Whole Wheat Linguine with Bacon and Baby Spinach

1	whole wheat linguine	3	Tbs	chopped fresh sage leaves, or to taste
1/4 lb	bacon, diced	1/2 lb		baby spinach leaves
1	onion, finely diced			salt and freshly ground pepper
1 1/3	cups chicken stock			grated Parmesan cheese

Procedure

1. Cook pasta according to package directions.
2. In large skillet over medium heat, cook bacon 4-5 minutes or until desired crispness; remove from pan, dice and return bacon to pan.
3. Add onion and sauté 5-6 minutes or until onion is tender. Stir in chicken stock and sage; simmer 1-2 minutes. Add spinach and cook until spinach just wilts.
4. Salt and pepper to taste.
5. Toss linguine with sauce and serve sprinkled with Parmesan cheese.

Servings: 4

Nutrition Facts

Serving size: 1/4 of a recipe (10.7 ounces).
Percent daily values based on the Reference Daily Intake (RDI) for a 2000 calorie diet.
Nutrition information calculated from recipe ingredients.

Amount Per Serving	
Calories	535.73
Calories From Fat (29%)	157.56
	% Daily Value
Total Fat 17.56g	27%
Saturated Fat 6.27g	31%
Cholesterol 30.02mg	10%
Sodium 523.55mg	22%
Potassium 454.6mg	13%
Total Carbohydrates 73.51g	25%
Fiber 4.08g	16%
Sugar 3.98g	
Protein 20.54g	41%

Yummy Black Bean Burritos

Easy and yummy!

4		10-inch flour tortillas
1/4 cup		vegetable oil
1		small onion, chopped
1		red bell pepper, chopped
2	tsp	minced garlic

2	tsp	minced jalapeno pepper
2		15-ounce cans black beans, rinsed and drained
6	oz	cream cheese
1	tsp	salt
1/4 cup		chopped fresh cilantro

Procedure

1. Preheat oven to 350°. Wrap tortillas in foil and place in heated oven. Bake for 15 minutes or until heated through.

2. Heat oil in a 10-inch skillet over medium heat. Place onion, bell pepper, garlic and jalapenos in skillet, cook for 2 minutes stirring occasionally. Pour beans into skillet, cook 3 minutes, stirring.

3. Cut cream cheese into cubes and add to skillet with salt. Cook for 2 minutes, stirring occasionally. Stir cilantro into mixture. Spoon mixture evenly down center of warmed tortilla and roll tortillas. Serve immediately.

Servings: 4

Nutrition Facts

Serving size: 1/4 of a recipe (12.4 ounces).
Percent daily values based on the Reference Daily Intake (RDI) for a 2000 calorie diet.
Nutrition information calculated from recipe ingredients.

Amount Per Serving	
Calories	557.33
Calories From Fat (63%)	349.68
	% Daily Value
Total Fat 31.82g	49%
Saturated Fat 10.94g	55%
Cholesterol 46.78mg	16%
Sodium 1589.08mg	66%
Potassium 229.4mg	7%
Total Carbohydrates 23.09g	8%
Fiber 12.65g	51%
Sugar 4.8g	
Protein 18.6g	37%

Salads & Sides

Make simple dinners extravagant with these side dishes.

The only real stumbling block is fear of failure.
In cooking you've got to have a
'What the hell?' attitude.

~Julia Child

5 Bean Salad

1		can (15 oz) green beans, drained	3		onions, medium, sliced thin
1		can (15 oz) yellow beans, drained	1	cup	vinegar
1		can (10 oz) lima beans, drained	1/2	cup	sugar
1		can (15 oz) garbanzo beans, drained	1/4	cup	canola oil
1		can (15 oz) red kidney beans, drained	1	tsp	salt
1		Green pepper, slivered	1/2	tsp	pepper
4		celery stalks, sliced			

Procedure

1. Combine sugar, salt and vinegar in pan. Bring to a boil for 1 min. Cool completely. Toss all other ingredients together and pour the vinegar mixture over them.

2. Marinate for 24 hrs in refrigerator, stirring occasionally.

Servings: 8

Nutrition Facts

Serving size: 1/8 of a recipe (7.3 ounces).
Percent daily values based on the Reference Daily Intake (RDI) for a 2000 calorie diet.
Nutrition information calculated from recipe ingredients.

Amount Per Serving	
Calories	161.07
Calories From Fat (38%)	61.06
	% Daily Value
Total Fat 7.04g	11%
Saturated Fat 0.54g	3%
Cholesterol 0mg	0%
Sodium 497.04mg	21%
Potassium 276.29mg	8%
Total Carbohydrates 25.06g	8%
Fiber 2.69g	11%
Sugar 15.85g	
Protein 1.96g	4%

Barley Casserole

1/4 cup	butter		1/2 cup	sliced fresh mushrooms
1	medium onion, diced		1/2 cup	fresh parsley, chopped
1 cup	uncooked pearl barley		1/4 tsp	salt
1/2 cup	pine nuts		1/8 tsp	pepper
2	green onions, thinly sliced		2	14.5-ounce cans chicken broth

Procedure

1. Preheat oven to 350°.
2. Melt butter in a skillet over medium-high heat. Stir in onion, barley and pine nuts. Cook and stir until barley is lightly browned. Mix in green onions, mushrooms and parsley. Season with salt and pepper.
3. Transfer the mixture to a 2 quart casserole dish, and stir in the vegetable broth. Bake 1 hour and 15 minutes in preheated oven, or until liquid has been absorbed and barley is tender.

Servings: 6

Nutrition Facts

Serving size: 1/6 of a recipe (8.1 ounces).
Percent daily values based on the Reference Daily Intake (RDI) for a 2000 calorie diet.
Nutrition information calculated from recipe ingredients.

Amount Per Serving	
Calories	296.65
Calories From Fat (48%)	143.37
	% Daily Value
Total Fat 16.63g	26%
Saturated Fat 5.73g	29%
Cholesterol 20.34mg	7%
Sodium 550.2mg	23%
Potassium 373.29mg	11%
Total Carbohydrates 30.89g	10%
Fiber 6.28g	25%
Sugar 1.82g	
Protein 8.37g	17%

Broccoli with Garlic Butter

1 1/2	lbs	fresh broccoli, cut into bite-size pieces	2	tsp	white vinegar
1/3 cup		butter	1/4 tsp		ground black pepper
1	Tbs	brown sugar	2		cloves garlic, minced
3	Tbs	soy sauce			

Procedure

1 Place the broccoli into a large pot with about 1 inch of water in the bottom. Bring to a boil and cook for 7 minutes, or until tender but still crisp. Drain, and arrange broccoli on a serving platter.

2 While the broccoli is cooking, melt the butter in a small skillet over medium heat. Mix in the brown sugar, soy sauce, vinegar, pepper and garlic. Bring to a boil; remove from the heat. Pour the sauce over the broccoli. Serve immediately.

Servings: 6

Nutrition Facts

Serving size: 1/6 of a recipe (4.7 ounces).
Percent daily values based on the Reference Daily Intake (RDI) for a 2000 calorie diet.
Nutrition information calculated from recipe ingredients.

Amount Per Serving	
Calories	135.6
Calories From Fat (69%)	92.97
	% Daily Value
Total Fat 10.62g	**16%**
Saturated Fat 6.54g	**33%**
Cholesterol 27.11mg	**9%**
Sodium 331.23mg	**14%**
Potassium 380.06mg	**11%**
Total Carbohydrates 9.07g	**3%**
Fiber 0.12g	**<1%**
Sugar 2.38g	
Protein 3.82g	**8%**

Cabbage Salad

1	small head cabbage firm, shredded	½	medium green bell pepper, diced
1	large carrot, shredded	4	green onions, thinly sliced
2 cups	cauliflower, separated and steamed until tender, but not soft	1/2 cup	raisins
			dressing (see below)

Procedure

1. Combine ingredients in a large bowl. Add dressing to taste.

Servings: 5

Tips

Try Organic Raspberry Vinaigrette Dressing from the health food section of your supermarket.

Nutrition Facts

Serving size: 1/5 of a recipe (4.5 ounces).
Percent daily values based on the Reference Daily Intake (RDI) for a 2000 calorie diet.
Nutrition information calculated from recipe ingredients.

Amount Per Serving	
Calories	78.63
Calories From Fat (4%)	3.41
	% Daily Value
Total Fat 0.41g	<1%
Saturated Fat 0.07g	<1%
Cholesterol 0mg	0%
Sodium 26.07mg	1%
Potassium 350.14mg	10%
Total Carbohydrates 19.25g	6%
Fiber 3.39g	14%
Sugar 12.49g	
Protein 2.18g	4%

California Bean Sprout Salad

1		red pepper	1	tsp	sugar
1	head	romaine lettuce, small head	1/4	Tbs	salt
1	head	leaf lettuce, small head	1/2	cup	cucumber, diced
1	cup	jicama, cut in 2-inch strips	1		avocado, cubed
2	cups	bean sprouts, cooked	1	tsp	sesame oil, optional
1		hard-boiled egg			
1/4	cup	cider vinegar			

Procedure

1. Prepare the red pepper — wash, cut in half and remove seeds and membranes; cut into small strips.
2. Wash lettuce, spin or blot dry and place in plastic bag with a paper towel; seal bag and refrigerate. Cut peeled jicama into french-fry size strips and refrigerate until serving time.
3. In saucepan, bring 1 quart water to a boil. Add the bean sprouts and blanch for two minutes. Remove and run under cold water briefly. Immerse in a bowl of ice water for one minute; drain well. Mash boiled egg or put through a sieve. Refrigerate.
4. In a small bowl, blend vinegar, sugar and salt. In a large bowl, combine bean sprouts, diced cucumbers, strips of red pepper and avocado cubes. Add 1 teaspoon of sesame oil if desired and blend this mixture well.
5. Add the vinegar mixture to the bean sprout mixture and toss to combine. Cover bowl tightly and refrigerate 1 hour.
6. To serve, tear lettuce into bite-size pieces and divide equally among 4-6 salad plates. Top with the sprout mixture, sprinkle with the chopped egg, and arrange the jicama strips on one side of salad. Needs no further dressing to be a delicious and healthy dish.

Servings: 4

Nutrition Facts

Serving size: 1/4 of a recipe (13.2 ounces).
Percent daily values based on the Reference Daily Intake (RDI) for a 2000 calorie diet.
Nutrition information calculated from recipe ingredients.

Amount Per Serving	
Calories	171.51
Calories From Fat (49%)	84.34
	% Daily Value
Total Fat 9.97g	15%
Saturated Fat 1.65g	8%
Cholesterol 60.29mg	20%
Sodium 625.14mg	26%
Potassium 836.71mg	24%
Total Carbohydrates 18.45g	6%
Fiber 8.94g	36%
Sugar 7g	
Protein 6.46g	13%

Chicken Salad Nouveau

2	cups	cooked chicken, chopped
1/2 cup		Monterey jack cheese, shredded
1/2 cup		cheddar cheese, shredded
1		avocado, diced
1/2 cup		olives, chopped
1		tomatillos, chopped
1/2 tsp		chili powder

1/4 tsp		garlic powder
1	tsp	onions, chopped
		black pepper
2	Tbs	mayonnaise
1	tsp	green chilies, minced
2	tsp	sun-dried tomatoes, oil-packed, minced
		tortilla chips

Procedure

1. Lightly mix the first 10 ingredients together. Moisten with mayonnaise, using more or less as desired. Mound in 4 decorative serving dishes; sprinkle the minced green chilies and minced sun-dried tomatoes on top. Chill for 1 hour. Serve with corn chips or crisp-fried tortillas as a light lunch.

Servings: 4

Nutrition Facts

Serving size: 1/4 of a recipe (6.3 ounces).
Percent daily values based on the Reference Daily Intake (RDI) for a 2000 calorie diet.
Nutrition information calculated from recipe ingredients.

Amount Per Serving	
Calories	352.68
Calories From Fat (56%)	196.48
	% Daily Value
Total Fat 22.64g	**35%**
Saturated Fat 7.93g	**40%**
Cholesterol 88.81mg	**30%**
Sodium 426.57mg	**18%**
Potassium 477.26mg	**14%**
Total Carbohydrates 8.02g	**3%**
Fiber 3.87g	**15%**
Sugar 1.18g	
Protein 29.94g	**60%**

Chickpea Salad

1	15 oz can	chickpeas (garbanzo beans), drained and rinsed
1		cucumber, peeled and finely chopped
1	cup	grape tomatoes, halved
1/4 cup		finely chopped sweet onion

1	Tbs	minced garlic
1/2 tsp		dried parsley flakes
1/4 tsp		dried basil
1	Tbs	Parmesan cheese, grated
1	Tbs	olive oil
3	Tbs	balsamic vinegar
1/4 tsp		salt

Procedure

1. In a large bowl, toss together chickpeas, cucumber, tomatoes, onion, garlic, parsley flakes, dried basil and Parmesan cheese. Drizzle with olive oil and balsamic vinegar. Season to taste with salt. Toss until well combined, and adjust seasoning as needed. Cover and refrigerate at least 45 minutes before serving. Serve chilled.

Servings: 4

Nutrition Facts

Serving size: 1/4 of a recipe (9.1 ounces).
Percent daily values based on the Reference Daily Intake (RDI) for a 2000 calorie diet.
Nutrition information calculated from recipe ingredients.

Amount Per Serving	
Calories	194.62
Calories From Fat (23%)	45.61
	% Daily Value
Total Fat 5.28g	8%
Saturated Fat 0.82g	4%
Cholesterol 1.1mg	<1%
Sodium 507.29mg	21%
Potassium 421.19mg	12%
Total Carbohydrates 31.1g	10%
Fiber 6.06g	24%
Sugar 1.11g	
Protein 7.06g	14%

Foil Wrapped Sweet Potatoes and Veggies

2 1/2	lbs	new potatoes, thinly sliced	1		sprig fresh thyme
2		large sweet potatoes, thinly sliced	2	Tbs	olive oil
2		Vidalia onions, sliced 1/4 inch thick			salt to taste
1/2 lb		fresh green beans, cut into 1 inch pieces			pepper to taste
1		sprig fresh rosemary	1/4 cup		olive oil

Procedure

1. Preheat grill for high heat.
2. In a large bowl, combine the new potatoes, sweet potato, Vidalia onions, green beans, rosemary, and thyme. Stir in 2 tablespoons olive oil, salt, and pepper to coat.
3. Using 2 to 3 layers of foil, create desired number of foil packets. Brush inside surfaces of packets liberally with remaining olive oil. Distribute vegetable mixture evenly among the packets. Seal tightly. Place packets on preheated grill. Cook 30 minutes, turning once, or until potatoes are tender.

Servings: 8

Nutrition Facts

Serving size: 1/8 of a recipe (8.6 ounces).
Percent daily values based on the Reference Daily Intake (RDI) for a 2000 calorie diet.
Nutrition information calculated from recipe ingredients.

Amount Per Serving	
Calories	282.97
Calories From Fat (32%)	90.46
	% Daily Value
Total Fat 10.24g	**16%**
Saturated Fat 1.4g	7%
Cholesterol 0mg	0%
Sodium 48.69mg	2%
Potassium 1188.03mg	34%
Total Carbohydrates 45.55g	15%
Fiber 4.57g	18%
Sugar 2.67g	
Protein 4.8g	10%

Garlic Potatoes

2	lbs	red potatoes, quartered	1	tsp	salt
1/4 cup		butter, melted	1		lemon, juiced
2	cloves	garlic, minced	1	Tbs	Parmesan cheese, grated

Procedure

1. Preheat oven to 350°.
2. Place potatoes in an 8x8 inch baking dish. In a small bowl, combine melted butter, garlic, salt and lemon juice; pour over potatoes and stir to coat. Sprinkle Parmesan cheese over potatoes.
3. Bake, covered, in preheated oven for 30 minutes. Uncover and bake an additional 10 minutes, or until golden brown.

Servings: 4

Nutrition Facts

Serving size: 1/4 of a recipe (9.2 ounces).
Percent daily values based on the Reference Daily Intake (RDI) for a 2000 calorie diet.
Nutrition information calculated from recipe ingredients.

Amount Per Serving	
Calories	292.21
Calories From Fat (36%)	106.24
	% Daily Value
Total Fat 12.08g	**19%**
Saturated Fat 7.54g	**38%**
Cholesterol 31.6mg	**11%**
Sodium 616.05mg	**26%**
Potassium 1260.96mg	**36%**
Total Carbohydrates 42.59g	**14%**
Fiber 3.72g	**15%**
Sugar 0.39g	
Protein 5.44g	**11%**

Glazed Carrots

5		carrots, sliced	1 1/2 Tbs honey	
2	Tbs	butter	1/4 cup dried cherries	

Procedure

1. Bring one inch of water in a medium saucepan to a boil. Add carrots and cook until tender, about 10 minutes. Drain carrots and remove from the pan; set aside.

2. In the same pan, melt the butter over medium heat. Stir in the honey until dissolved. Add the cherries and simmer over low heat for one minute. Remove from heat and stir in carrots until completely coated.

Servings: 4

Nutrition Facts

Serving size: 1/4 of a recipe (4.4 ounces).
Percent daily values based on the Reference Daily Intake (RDI) for a 2000 calorie diet.
Nutrition information calculated from recipe ingredients.

Amount Per Serving	
Calories	146.3
Calories From Fat (37%)	53.68
	% Daily Value
Total Fat 6.12g	9%
Saturated Fat 3.68g	18%
Cholesterol 15.27mg	5%
Sodium 72.1mg	3%
Potassium 329.3mg	9%
Total Carbohydrates 23.68g	8%
Fiber 3.35g	13%
Sugar 11.06g	
Protein 1.27g	3%

Grilled Artichokes

This recipe will make an artichoke fan out of anyone!

2		artichokes, halved and choke scraped out	2		cloves garlic, chopped
2	tsp	sea salt	1		shallot, chopped
1	tsp	ground black pepper	1/2 cup	butter

Procedure

1. Preheat an outdoor grill for low heat.
2. Meanwhile, bring a large pot of water to a boil. Place the artichokes into the boiling water, and season with salt and pepper. Throw in half of the garlic and half of the shallot. Boil for about 30 minutes, or until a fork is easily inserted into the stem of the artichokes. Drain and set aside.
3. Melt the butter in a small pan over medium heat, and stir in the remaining garlic and shallot. Cook just until fragrant, and then remove from the heat.
4. Place the artichoke halves onto preheated grill. Brush some of the melted butter onto them. Cook for 5 to 10 minutes, brushing with butter occasionally, until lightly toasted. Serve with remaining butter as a dipping sauce.

Servings: 4

Nutrition Facts

Serving size: 1/4 of a recipe (11.7 ounces).
Percent daily values based on the Reference Daily Intake (RDI) for a 2000 calorie diet.
Nutrition information calculated from recipe ingredients.

Amount Per Serving	
Calories	377.53
Calories From Fat (54%)	205.62
	% Daily Value
Total Fat 23.44g	36%
Saturated Fat 14.6g	73%
Cholesterol 61.01mg	20%
Sodium 1144.01mg	48%
Potassium 1052.61mg	30%
Total Carbohydrates 39.67g	13%
Fiber 10.87g	43%
Sugar 0.04g	
Protein 9.78g	20%

Mashed Artichoke Potatoes

4		large baking potatoes, peeled and quartered	1/4 cup softened butter
1		15-ounce can artichoke hearts in water, drained	sea salt
1	tsp	minced garlic, or to taste	black pepper
1/2 cup		hot milk	

Procedure

1. Place potatoes in a large pot with enough water to cover. Bring to a boil over high heat; reduce heat to medium-low. Cover and simmer until tender, 15 to 20 minutes; drain.

2. Meanwhile, puree the artichokes and garlic with the milk until smooth.

3. Place drained potatoes in a mixing bowl and mash with a potato masher until smooth. Stir in softened butter and artichoke puree until the butter has melted. Season to taste with salt and pepper.

Servings: 4

Nutrition Facts

Serving size: 1/4 of a recipe (9.4 ounces).
Percent daily values based on the Reference Daily Intake (RDI) for a 2000 calorie diet.
Nutrition information calculated from recipe ingredients.

Amount Per Serving	
Calories	290.69
Calories From Fat (37%)	107.77
	% Daily Value
Total Fat 12.26g	19%
Saturated Fat 7.67g	38%
Cholesterol 32.94mg	11%
Sodium 186.96mg	8%
Potassium 1246.53mg	36%
Total Carbohydrates 41.78g	14%
Fiber 7.37g	29%
Sugar 1.56g	
Protein 7.63g	15%

Succulent Spinach

Fresh spinach is perfect for this dish, though you may use frozen.

1		shallot, minced	2		bags of baby spinach
4	Tbs	butter	1/2 cup		chicken stock
4		garlic cloves, crushed	1	cup	Panko bread crumbs
1	Tbs	all-purpose flour			salt
1		10.75-ounce can condensed cream of celery soup			pepper

Procedure

1. Preheat oven to 350°.
2. Chop spinach 1 to 2 inches thick and set aside.
3. In a saucepan, sauté 1 minced shallot and 4 crushed cloves of garlic with butter until tender. Add 1 tablespoon of flour and let cook slightly. Slowly stir in soup. Cook until thickened. Thin to your liking with ¼ to ½ cup of chicken stock. Remove from heat.
4. Fold chopped spinach gently into the sauce mixture and place in 13 x 9 buttered dish. Top with bread crumbs and season with salt and pepper.
5. Bake for 15 minute or to slightly crisp topping.

Servings: 4

Nutrition Facts

Serving size: 1/4 of a recipe (14.4 ounces).
Percent daily values based on the Reference Daily Intake (RDI) for a 2000 calorie diet.
Nutrition information calculated from recipe ingredients.

Amount Per Serving	
Calories	339.53
Calories From Fat (42%)	141.22
	% Daily Value
Total Fat 16.08g	25%
Saturated Fat 8.37g	42%
Cholesterol 39.82mg	13%
Sodium 829.67mg	35%
Potassium 1403.33mg	40%
Total Carbohydrates 42.23g	14%
Fiber 4.82g	19%
Sugar 3.76g	
Protein 11.12g	22%

Sweet Sweet Potatoes

3		large sweet potatoes	1	Tbs	orange juice
3	Tbs	butter			dash cinnamon
1/2 cup		sugar brown sugar, packed	2	cups	marshmallows (optional for you, not for me)

Procedure

1. Preheat oven to 350°. Peel skin off of potatoes and cut into thick chunks. Boil for about 30 minutes or until tender. Drain and place in a baking pan.

2. In a medium saucepan melt butter. Stir in butter, brown sugar, and orange juice. Pour mixture over potatoes. Top with marshmallows.

3. Bake in oven for 10 minutes or until marshmallows have slightly melted and are a warm brown color.

Servings: 4

Nutrition Facts

Serving size: 1/4 of a recipe (7.7 ounces).
Percent daily values based on the Reference Daily Intake (RDI) for a 2000 calorie diet.
Nutrition information calculated from recipe ingredients.

Amount Per Serving	
Calories	445.77
Calories From Fat (18%)	78.61
	% Daily Value
Total Fat 8.96g	**14%**
Saturated Fat 5.54g	**28%**
Cholesterol 22.9mg	**8%**
Sodium 45.58mg	**2%**
Potassium 1361.89mg	**39%**
Total Carbohydrates 91.14g	**30%**
Fiber 6.24g	**25%**
Sugar 43.75g	
Protein 2.97g	**6%**

Thyme Potatoes

3	lbs	russet or Yukon Gold potatoes, peeled, quartered		6	Tbs	(or more) warm whipping cream
4 1/2		Tbs butter, room temperature		1 1/2		Tbs minced fresh thyme

Procedure

1. Boil potatoes until tender, about 20 minutes. Drain; return to pot.
2. Add butter, 6 tablespoons cream and thyme; mash. Season with salt and pepper.

Servings: 6

Nutrition Facts

Serving size: 1/6 of a recipe (8.9 ounces).
Percent daily values based on the Reference Daily Intake (RDI) for a 2000 calorie diet.
Nutrition information calculated from recipe ingredients.

Amount Per Serving	
Calories	310.25
Calories From Fat (41%)	127.01
	% Daily Value
Total Fat 14.45g	**22%**
Saturated Fat 9g	**45%**
Cholesterol 43.45mg	**14%**
Sodium 18.8mg	**<1%**
Potassium 968.31mg	**28%**
Total Carbohydrates 42.1g	**14%**
Fiber 3.35g	**13%**
Sugar 1.45g	
Protein 5.35g	**11%**

Wild Rice Casserole

2		14.5-ounce cans chicken broth	1	tsp	salt
1	cup	uncooked wild rice	1/2 lb		fresh mushrooms, sliced
1/2 cup		water chestnuts, sliced	1/2 cup		onion, chopped
1/4 cup		butter			

Procedure

1. Preheat oven to 350°. Bring chicken broth to a boil in a medium saucepan.
2. In a 1 1/2 quart baking dish, mix chicken broth, uncooked wild rice, water chestnuts, 2 tablespoons butter and salt.
3. Cover. Bake in preheated oven 30 minutes.
4. While rice mixture is baking, melt remaining butter in a medium skillet over medium heat. Place mushrooms and onion in skillet and slowly cook and stir until tender. Stir mushrooms and onion into the wild rice mixture, cover and continue baking 30 minutes, or until liquid has been absorbed.

Servings: 6

Nutrition Facts

Serving size: 1/6 of a recipe (8.5 ounces).
Percent daily values based on the Reference Daily Intake (RDI) for a 2000 calorie diet.
Nutrition information calculated from recipe ingredients.

Amount Per Serving	
Calories	205.13
Calories From Fat (38%)	78.65
	% Daily Value
Total Fat 8.9g	**14%**
Saturated Fat 5.15g	**26%**
Cholesterol 20.34mg	**7%**
Sodium 837.87mg	**35%**
Potassium 388.1mg	**11%**
Total Carbohydrates 24.52g	**8%**
Fiber 2.59g	**10%**
Sugar 2.23g	
Protein 8.23g	**16%**

Wild Rice with Cranberries

Throw in some grilled chicken and you have a complete meal.

1/2 cup	(1 stick) butter	
2	large onions, chopped	
1	garlic clove, minced	
6 3/4	cups canned low-salt chicken broth	
2	cups wild rice (about 13 ounces)	
2	cups long-grain brown rice	

2	cups dried cranberries	
1/2 cup	fresh parsley, chopped	
2	Tbs fresh thyme, chopped	
1 1/2	cups hazelnuts, toasted, husked, coarsely chopped	
1	cup green onions, chopped	

Procedure

1. Melt butter in heavy large pot over medium-high heat. Add onions and garlic and sauté until tender, about 4 minutes. Add chicken broth. Bring to boil.

2. Add wild rice. Reduce heat to medium-low. Cover and simmer 30 minutes. Mix in brown rice; cover and simmer until rice is just tender and most liquid is absorbed, about 30 minutes longer.

3. Stir cranberries, parsley and thyme into rice. Cover and cook until liquid is absorbed, about 5 minutes longer. Mix in hazelnuts and green onions. Season generously with salt and pepper.

4. If you want to use rice as stuffing in turkey: Loosely fill main cavity with stuffing. Butter ceramic baking dish. Spoon remaining stuffing into prepared dish. Cover with buttered foil, buttered side down. Bake stuffing in dish alongside turkey until heated through, about 30 minutes. To bake all of stuffing in baking dish: Preheat oven to 350°. Butter 15x10x2-inch glass or ceramic baking dish. Transfer stuffing to prepared dish. Cover dish with buttered foil, buttered side down; bake stuffing until heated through, about 40 minutes.

Servings: 14

Nutrition Facts

Serving size: 1/14 of a recipe (11 ounces).
Percent daily values based on the Reference Daily Intake (RDI) for a 2000 calorie diet.
Nutrition information calculated from recipe ingredients.

Amount Per Serving	
Calories	558.51
Calories From Fat (25%)	137.36
	% Daily Value
Total Fat 15.98g	25%
Saturated Fat 4.83g	24%
Cholesterol 17.43mg	6%
Sodium 277.54mg	12%
Potassium 395.57mg	11%
Total Carbohydrates 98.4g	33%
Fiber 9.36g	37%
Sugar 2.15g	
Protein 7.99g	16%

Soups

These hearty soups can be eaten as a meal.

Soup is liquid comfort.
~Author Unknown

Beef Barley Soup

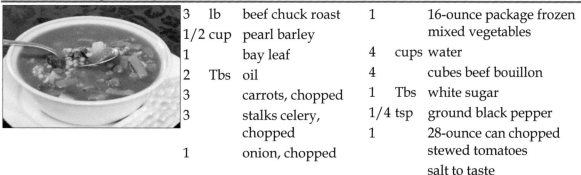

3	lb	beef chuck roast	1		16-ounce package frozen mixed vegetables
1/2	cup	pearl barley			
1		bay leaf	4	cups	water
2	Tbs	oil	4		cubes beef bouillon
3		carrots, chopped	1	Tbs	white sugar
3		stalks celery, chopped	1/4	tsp	ground black pepper
1		onion, chopped	1		28-ounce can chopped stewed tomatoes
					salt to taste

Procedure

1. In a slow cooker, cook chuck roast until very tender (usually 4 to 5 hours on high, but can vary with different slow cookers). Add barley and bay leaf during the last hour of cooking. Remove meat and chop into bite-size pieces. Discard bay leaf. Set beef, broth and barley aside.

2. Heat oil in a large stock pot over medium-high heat. Sauté carrots, celery, onion, and frozen mixed vegetables until tender. Add water, beef bouillon cubes, sugar, 1/4 teaspoon pepper, chopped stewed tomatoes, and beef/barley mixture. Bring to boil; reduce heat and simmer 10 to 20 minutes. Season with additional salt and pepper to taste.

Servings: 10

Nutrition Facts

Serving size: 1/10 of a recipe (10.8 ounces).
Percent daily values based on the Reference Daily Intake (RDI) for a 2000 calorie diet.
Nutrition information calculated from recipe ingredients.

Amount Per Serving	
Calories	229.73
Calories From Fat (46%)	105.53
	% Daily Value
Total Fat 11.79g	18%
Saturated Fat 4.03g	20%
Cholesterol 25.59mg	9%
Sodium 524.05mg	22%
Potassium 472.18mg	13%
Total Carbohydrates 22.92g	8%
Fiber 4.7g	19%
Sugar 7.29g	
Protein 9.74g	19%

Butternut Squash Soup

6	cups	butternut squash	4		cubes chicken bouillon
1/2	cup	onion, chopped	1/2 tsp		dried marjoram
4	Tbs	butter	1/4 tsp		ground black pepper
3	cups	water	1/8 tsp		ground cayenne pepper
1		Granny Smith apple	4	oz	(1/2 package) cream cheese

Procedure

1. Preheat oven to 375°. Cut squash in half and place cut side down on a baking sheet. Bake for 45 minutes. Cut squash into cubes.

2. In a large saucepan, sauté onions in butter until tender. Add roasted squash, water, apple, bouillon, marjoram, black pepper and cayenne pepper. Bring to boil; reduce heat and cook an additional 20 minutes, until apple is tender.

3. Pour contents into a blender or food processor and puree squash and cream cheese until smooth. Return to saucepan and heat through. Do not allow to boil.

Servings: 6

Nutrition Facts

Serving size: 1/6 of a recipe.
Percent daily values based on the Reference Daily Intake (RDI) for a 2000 calorie diet.
Nutrition information provided by the recipe author.

Amount Per Serving	
Calories	236.26
Calories From Fat (53%)	124.84

	% Daily Value
Total Fat 14.87g	**23%**
Saturated Fat 9.15g	**46%**
Cholesterol 41.49mg	**14%**
Sodium 563.56mg	**23%**
Potassium 648.12mg	**19%**
Total Carbohydrates 25.91g	**9%**
Fiber 5.43g	**22%**
Sugar 6.35g	
Protein 3.95g	**8%**

Corn Chowder

6	red potatoes, peeled and cubed	1	Tbs	red pepper flakes
2	11-ounce cans whole kernel corn, undrained	2	cups	vegetable broth
1/2 cup	chopped green bell pepper	1		12-ounce package low-fat, firm silken tofu
1/2 cup	chopped sweet onion			salt to taste

Procedure

1. Place potatoes in a large pot of salted water and bring to a boil. Cook until tender, about 30 minutes; drain.

2. To the potatoes add corn, bell pepper, onion, red pepper flakes and vegetable broth. Boil for about 15 minutes; remove from heat.

3. In a food processor or blender puree all but 1 ½ cups of the vegetable and broth mixture with the tofu. Process in batches if necessary. Combine the pureed mixture with the remaining 1 ½ cups vegetable and broth mixture, and cook over low heat for 5 minutes; do not boil. Season with salt to taste.

Servings: 6

Nutrition Facts

Serving size: 1/6 of a recipe (12.4 ounces).
Percent daily values based on the Reference Daily Intake (RDI) for a 2000 calorie diet.
Nutrition information calculated from recipe ingredients.

Amount Per Serving	
Calories	226.55
Calories From Fat (14%)	31.73
	% Daily Value
Total Fat 3.74g	6%
Saturated Fat 0.75g	4%
Cholesterol 0.8mg	<1%
Sodium 460.84mg	19%
Potassium 984.73mg	28%
Total Carbohydrates 42.21g	14%
Fiber 4.4g	18%
Sugar 5.37g	
Protein 10g	20%

Granny's Ham and Bean Soup

1	lb	dry Great Northern beans	1	cup	chopped onion
3	cups	water	1	tsp	minced garlic
2		cans chicken broth	1	tsp	mustard powder
1		ham hock	2		bay leaves
1	cup	chopped carrots	2	cups	chopped ham
1/2		stalk celery, chopped	1/2 tsp		ground white pepper

Procedure

1. Rinse the beans, sorting out any broken or discolored ones. Soak in a bowl of water for 3-4 hours. Discard water in the morning. Add water and broth to a large soup pot and heat over high heat. Bring the water to a boil. Add the beans and remove from heat. Let beans sit in the hot water for at least 60 minutes.

2. After the 60 minutes of soaking, return the pot to high heat and place the ham bone, carrots, celery, onion, garlic, mustard and bay leaves in the pot. Bring to a boil, stirring well; reduce heat to low and simmer for 1 to 2 hours.

3. Remove ham bone and discard. Stir in the chopped ham and simmer for 30 more minutes. Season with ground white pepper to taste.

4. Crock pot directions: Soak beans overnight. Put all ingredients in crock pot and cook on high for 6 hours.

Servings: 8

Nutrition Facts

Serving size: 1/8 of a recipe (12.2 ounces).
Percent daily values based on the Reference Daily Intake (RDI) for a 2000 calorie diet.
Nutrition information calculated from recipe ingredients.

Amount Per Serving	
Calories	292.91
Calories From Fat (16%)	48.08
	% Daily Value
Total Fat 5.34g	**8%**
Saturated Fat 1.69g	**8%**
Cholesterol 57.02mg	**19%**
Sodium 993.96mg	**41%**
Potassium 1025.3mg	**29%**
Total Carbohydrates 33.44g	**11%**
Fiber 10.02g	**40%**
Sugar 3.21g	
Protein 27.65g	**55%**

Hearty Minestrone

This is great served with bread and a Caesar salad.

3	Tbs	olive oil	2	cups	baby spinach, rinsed
3		cloves garlic, chopped	3		zucchinis, quartered and sliced
2		onions, chopped			
2	cups	chopped celery	1	Tbs	chopped fresh oregano
5		carrots, sliced			
2	cups	chicken broth	2	Tbs	chopped fresh basil
2	cups	water			salt to taste
4	cups	tomato sauce			pepper
1/2	cup	red wine (optional)	1/2	cup	small seashell pasta
1	cup	canned kidney beans, drained	2	Tbs	grated Parmesan cheese for topping
1	15-oz	can green beans	1	Tbs	olive oil

Procedure

1. In a large stock pot, over medium-low heat, heat olive oil and sauté garlic for 2 to 3 minutes. Add onion and sauté for 4 to 5 minutes. Add celery and carrots; sauté for 1 to 2 minutes.

2. Add chicken broth, water and tomato sauce; bring to boil, stirring frequently. If desired, add red wine at this point. Reduce heat to low and add kidney beans, green beans, spinach leaves, zucchini, oregano, basil, salt and pepper. Simmer for 30 to 40 minutes, the longer the better.

3. Fill a medium saucepan with water and bring to a boil. Add pasta and cook until tender. Drain water and set aside.

4. Once pasta is cooked and soup is heated through place 2 tablespoons cooked pasta into individual serving bowls. Ladle soup on top of pasta and sprinkle Parmesan cheese on top. Spray with olive oil and serve.

Servings 8

Nutrition Facts

Serving size: 1/8 of a recipe (16.3 ounces).
Percent daily values based on the Reference Daily Intake (RDI) for a 2000 calorie diet.
Nutrition information calculated from recipe ingredients.

Amount Per Serving	
Calories	218.41
Calories From Fat (33%)	72.88
	% Daily Value
Total Fat 8.31g	13%
Saturated Fat 1.37g	7%
Cholesterol 1.1mg	<1%
Sodium 1134.32mg	47%
Potassium 972.55mg	28%
Total Carbohydrates 31.61g	11%
Fiber 7.51g	30%
Sugar 9.82g	
Protein 7.69g	15%

Lentil Soup

1/4 cup	olive oil		2	cups	dry lentils
1		onion, chopped	8	cups	water
2		carrots, diced	1		14.5-ounce can crushed tomatoes
2		stalks celery, chopped	1/2 cup		spinach, rinsed and thinly sliced
2		cloves garlic, minced	2	Tbs	vinegar
1	tsp	dried oregano			salt to taste
1		bay leaf			ground black pepper to taste
1	tsp	dried basil			

Procedure

1. In a large soup pot, heat oil over medium heat. Add onions, carrots and celery; cook and stir until onion is tender. Stir in garlic, oregano, bay leaf and basil; cook for 2 minutes.

2. Stir in lentils; add water and tomatoes. Bring to a boil. Reduce heat and simmer for at least 1 hour. When ready to serve, stir in spinach and cook until it wilts. Stir in vinegar and season to taste with salt and pepper, and more vinegar, if desired.

Servings: 6

Nutrition Facts

Serving size: 1/6 of a recipe (17.1 ounces).
Percent daily values based on the Reference Daily Intake (RDI) for a 2000 calorie diet.
Nutrition information calculated from recipe ingredients.

Amount Per Serving	
Calories	186.11
Calories From Fat (45%)	83.14
	% Daily Value
Total Fat 9.45g	15%
Saturated Fat 1.29g	6%
Cholesterol 0mg	0%
Sodium 224.17mg	9%
Potassium 487.08mg	14%
Total Carbohydrates 20.3g	7%
Fiber 7.05g	28%
Sugar 4.19g	
Protein 6.89g	14%

Roasted Asparagus Soup

Here is a perfect springtime soup. I like this because it seems rich like it would have butter and cream in it, but it doesn't. Its rich flavor comes from roasting the vegetables, the chicken broth and the process of blending them all together. I also like the way the lemon perks up the flavor and of course Tabasco always adds a little kick.

4	lbs	asparagus, trimmed and cut into 2-in pieces (4 bunches)	1/3 cup		olive oil
4		leeks, chopped (white & pale green parts only)	6	cups	low sodium chicken broth
5		whole garlic cloves	1		lemon
1		red jalapeno			Tabasco
					salt to taste
					pepper to taste

Procedure

1 Preheat oven to 425°.

2 Combine asparagus, leeks, garlic, jalapeno and olive oil in very large bowl. Toss to coat. Season with salt and pepper. Divide between two rimmed baking sheets or roasting pans. Roast vegetables until asparagus pieces are soft and leeks are golden. Stir occasionally and roast for about 45 minutes. Set aside and cool.

3 Blend in batches starting with ½ of the vegetables and add 3 cups broth. Blend until smooth and pour soup into a large pot. Repeat the process using remaining vegetables and broth. Warm soup over medium heat and season with lemon juice and Tabasco to taste. Thin with more broth by adding ½ cup broth at a time if you like your soup thinner. Season with salt and pepper to your taste.

Servings: 4

Nutrition Facts

Serving size: 1/4 of a recipe (34.5 ounces).
Percent daily values based on the Reference Daily Intake (RDI) for a 2000 calorie diet.
Nutrition information calculated from recipe ingredients.

Amount Per Serving	
Calories	356.29
Calories From Fat (51%)	183.16
	% Daily Value
Total Fat 20.99g	32%
Saturated Fat 3.31g	17%
Cholesterol 0mg	0%
Sodium 170.35mg	7%
Potassium 1375.3mg	39%
Total Carbohydrates 34.11g	11%
Fiber 11.01g	44%
Sugar 9.08g	
Protein 18.53g	37%

Sausage Soup

Great recipe to freeze and reheat without losing flavor.

1	lb	hot or mild turkey Italian sausage	1		14.5-ounce can Great Northern beans, undrained
2		cloves garlic, minced	1/2 cup		whole wheat rigatoni
4	14 oz	cans beef broth	2		large zucchini, cubed
2		14.5-ounce can Italian-style stewed tomatoes (for a fresher, healthier taste, cut fresh tomatoes)	2	cups	spinach, rinsed and torn
			1/4 tsp		ground black pepper
1	cup	sliced celery	1/4 tsp		salt
1	cup	sliced carrots			Parmesan cheese

Procedure

4 In a stockpot, brown sausage with garlic. Stir in broth, tomatoes, celery and carrots. Season with salt and pepper. Reduce heat; cover and simmer 15 minutes. Skim fat off of the top.

5 Stir in beans with liquid and zucchini. Cover and simmer another 15 minutes, or until zucchini is tender.

6 While the soup is simmering, cook rigatoni according to package directions. Drain and add noodles to mixture.

7 Remove soup from heat and add spinach. Replace lid, allowing the heat from the soup to cook the spinach leaves. Soup is ready to serve after 5 minutes. Top with Parmesan cheese.

Servings: 6

Nutrition Facts

Serving size: 1/6 of a recipe (30.4 ounces).
Percent daily values based on the Reference Daily Intake (RDI) for a 2000 calorie diet.
Nutrition information calculated from recipe ingredients.

Amount Per Serving	
Calories	595.75
Calories From Fat (44%)	262.07
	% Daily Value
Total Fat 29.13g	**45%**
Saturated Fat 10.25g	**51%**
Cholesterol 65.52mg	**22%**
Sodium 2427.24mg	**101%**
Potassium 1547.99mg	**44%**
Total Carbohydrates 59.34g	**20%**
Fiber 8.74g	**35%**
Sugar 18.4g	
Protein 27.12g	**54%**

Sweet Cabbage Soup

1 1/2	lbs	lean ground beef	1/4 cup		white sugar
2		14.5-ounce cans diced tomatoes	1 1/2	tsp	salt
1		8-ounce can tomato sauce	1/2 tsp		ground black pepper
4		cubes beef bouillon	2	quarts	water, divided
2		medium carrots, shredded	3		cloves garlic, finely chopped
1		onion, chopped	1		head cabbage, cored and cut into wedges
2	Tbs	white vinegar			

Procedure

1 Crumble the ground beef into a large pot. Add the diced tomatoes, tomato sauce, beef bouillon cubes, carrots, onion, vinegar, sugar, salt and pepper.

2 Pour in 1 quart of water; bring to a boil. Stir to break up the beef while heating. Once the soup comes to a boil, cover and simmer for 30 minutes over low heat.

3 Pour in another quart of water and return to a slow boil. Add garlic and cabbage. Simmer for 25 minutes, until cabbage is tender. Ladle into soup bowls to serve.

Servings: 4

Nutrition Facts

Serving size: 1/4 of a recipe (37.1 ounces). Percent daily values based on the Reference Daily Intake (RDI) for a 2000 calorie diet. Nutrition information calculated from recipe ingredients.

Amount Per Serving	
Calories	637.43
Calories From Fat (53%)	335.67
	% Daily Value
Total Fat 36.42g	56%
Saturated Fat 14.43g	72%
Cholesterol 127.94mg	43%
Sodium 2261.6mg	94%
Potassium 1570.41mg	45%
Total Carbohydrates 43.83g	15%
Fiber 7.38g	30%
Sugar 19.07g	
Protein 36.31g	73%

Desserts

Just like everything in life, moderation is the key to being healthy. We have included some delicious desserts for those of you with a sweet tooth and still managed to sneak in some fiber.

Stressed spelled backwards is desserts.
Coincidence? I think not!
~Author Unknown

Baked Apples with or without Cashews

4		firm cooking apples such as Granny Smith or Golden Delicious
8	Tbs	raisins
		dash cinnamon

½	cup	raw cashews (optional)
1	tsp	vanilla
1/4	cup	water

Procedure

1. Core apples and fill each of the centers with 2 tablespoons of raisins. Sprinkle with cinnamon. Bake at 350° for 45 minutes or until the apples are tender.

2. Ground cashews in a blender or food processor. Add water and vanilla. Drizzle topping over baked apples, and enjoy!

Servings: 4

Nutrition Facts

Serving size: 1/4 of a recipe (6.5 ounces).
Percent daily values based on the Reference Daily Intake (RDI) for a 2000 calorie diet.
Nutrition information calculated from recipe ingredients.

Amount Per Serving	
Calories	199.8
Calories From Fat (26%)	52.16
	% Daily Value
Total Fat 6.18g	10%
Saturated Fat 1.09g	5%
Cholesterol 0mg	0%
Sodium 5.27mg	<1%
Potassium 367.6mg	11%
Total Carbohydrates 36.96g	12%
Fiber 4.41g	18%
Sugar 25.94g	
Protein 3.19g	6%

Baked Pears with Cranberries

3	firm	pears	½	cup	dried cranberries
½	cup	pomegranate juice			

Procedure

1. Preheat oven to 375°. Cut pears into slices and place in an 8 x 8 baking dish. Pour pomegranate juice over the pears. Sprinkle cranberries over the top. Bake for 15-20 minutes.

Servings: 3

Nutrition Facts

Serving size: 1/3 of a recipe.
Percent daily values based on the Reference Daily Intake (RDI) for a 2000 calorie diet.
Nutrition information provided by the recipe author.

Amount Per Serving	
Calories	197
Calories From Fat (23%)	44.82
	% Daily Value
Total Fat 5g	8%
Saturated Fat 0.4g	2%
Cholesterol 0mg	0%
Sodium 4mg	<1%
Potassium 0mg	0%
Total Carbohydrates 36.7g	12%
Fiber 4g	16%
Sugar 29g	
Protein 1.5g	3%

Berries & Cream

You can find lemon verbena, an herb, at many farmer's markets and health food stores. Lemon verbena is believed to have soothing properties and has been used to relieve digestive track spasms.

1/4 cup	water	
1/4 cup	plus 2 tablespoons sugar	
3 Tbs	chopped fresh lemon verbena leaves, divided	
2 Tbs	plus 1 cup chilled whipping cream	

4 cups assorted fresh berries (such as raspberries, blueberries, and boysenberries)

Additional sugar

Procedure

1. Mix ¼ cup water, ¼ cup sugar and 1 tablespoon lemon verbena in small saucepan. Bring to simmer over medium-high heat, stirring until sugar dissolves.

2. Cover and cool completely. Strain syrup into bowl.

3. Mix 2 tablespoons cream, 2 tablespoons sugar and 2 tablespoons lemon verbena in small saucepan. Bring to simmer over medium heat, stirring until sugar dissolves. Cover and let cool 30 minutes. Strain into small bowl; chill.

4. Stir in remaining 1 cup chilled cream. Whip verbena cream in medium bowl until peaks form. Divide whipped verbena cream among 4 small bowls. Toss berries and verbena syrup in large bowl.

5. Divide berries among 4 plates. Sprinkle with sugar and serve with whipped verbena cream. (Verbena syrup and verbena cream can be made 1 day ahead. Cover and refrigerate.)

Servings: 6

Nutrition Facts

Serving size: 1/6 of a recipe (6.7 ounces).
Percent daily values based on the Reference Daily Intake (RDI) for a 2000 calorie diet.
Nutrition information calculated from recipe ingredients.

Amount Per Serving	
Calories	362.95
Calories From Fat (72%)	261.72
	% Daily Value
Total Fat 29.78g	46%
Saturated Fat 18.29g	91%
Cholesterol 108.69mg	36%
Sodium 31.24mg	1%
Potassium 158.84mg	5%
Total Carbohydrates 24.54g	8%
Fiber 3.83g	15%
Sugar 17.14g	
Protein 2.48g	5%

Chocolate Cherry Caramel Apples

Chocolate really goes with everything, doesn't it?

6		Granny Smith apples	2	Tbs	water
6		wooden sticks	1/2	tsp	vanilla extract
1	cup	semisweet chocolate chips	1 1/2		cups dried cherries
1		14-ounce package individually wrapped caramels, unwrapped	1	cup	sliced almonds (optional)

Procedure

1. Insert wooden sticks 3/4 of the way into the stem end of each apple. Place apples on a cookie sheet covered with lightly greased aluminum foil. Place the chocolate chips into a small saucepan and melt on low heat. Set aside.

2. Combine caramels and water in a saucepan over low heat. Cook, stirring often, until caramel melts and is smooth. Stir in the vanilla. Dip each apple into the caramel and gently run apples around insides of saucepan to scrape off some of the caramel. Scrape excess caramel from the apple bottoms using the side of the saucepan.

3. Roll apples in mixture of cherries and almonds. Place on the aluminum foil. Use a spoon to drizzle chocolate over the apples. If the chocolate is too thick, thin by mixing with a little vegetable oil. Chill until ready to serve.

Servings: 6

Nutrition Facts

Serving size: 1/6 of a recipe (10.5 ounces).
Percent daily values based on the Reference Daily Intake (RDI) for a 2000 calorie diet.
Nutrition information calculated from recipe ingredients.

Amount Per Serving	
Calories	716.89
Calories From Fat (31%)	220.82
	% Daily Value
Total Fat 26.63g	**41%**
Saturated Fat 10.29g	**51%**
Cholesterol 4.63mg	**2%**
Sodium 171.88mg	**7%**
Potassium 461.32mg	**13%**
Total Carbohydrates 122.22g	**41%**
Fiber 10.47g	**42%**
Sugar 58.84g	
Protein 10.65g	**21%**

Banana Chocolate Chip Bread Pudding

4		eggs	4	cups cubed french bread
2	cups	milk	3	bananas, lightly mashed
1/2	cup	white sugar	2	cup semisweet chocolate chips
1	Tbs	vanilla extract	1	dash cinnamon

Procedure

1. Preheat oven to 350°. Grease a 9x5 inch loaf pan.
2. In a large mixing bowl, mix eggs, milk, sugar and vanilla until smooth. Stir in bread, bananas, chocolate chips and cinnamon and let rest 5 minutes for bread to soak. Pour into prepared pan.
3. Line a roasting pan with a damp kitchen towel. Place loaf pan on towel inside roasting pan, and place roasting pan on oven rack. Fill roasting pan with water to reach halfway up the sides of the loaf pan. Bake in preheated oven for 1 hour, or until a knife inserted in the center comes out clean.

Servings: 6

Nutrition Facts

Serving size: 1/6 of a recipe (13.6 ounces).
Percent daily values based on the Reference Daily Intake (RDI) for a 2000 calorie diet.
Nutrition information calculated from recipe ingredients.

Amount Per Serving	
Calories	839.95
Calories From Fat (25%)	213.66
	% Daily Value
Total Fat 25.78g	40%
Saturated Fat 12.89g	64%
Cholesterol 147.51mg	49%
Sodium 866.57mg	36%
Potassium 558.4mg	16%
Total Carbohydrates 138.49g	46%
Fiber 8.92g	36%
Sugar 29.92g	
Protein 21.23g	42%

Chocolate PB Bars

1	cup	butter, softened		2	cups	rolled oats
1	cup	white sugar		2	cups	all-purpose flour
1	cup	brown sugar		1	tsp	baking soda
2		eggs		2 1/2		cups semisweet chocolate chips
3/4 cup		peanut butter		1/2 cup		peanut butter

Procedure

1. Preheat oven to 350°. Grease a 9x13 inch baking pan. In a large bowl, cream together butter, white sugar and brown sugar. Beat in eggs, one at a time, then stir in peanut butter. Combine oats, flour and baking soda; stir into the creamed mixture until well blended. Press the dough evenly into the prepared pan.

2. Bake for 15 to 20 minutes in preheated oven, until firm. In the microwave or over a double boiler, melt chocolate chips and 1/2 cup peanut butter together, stirring frequently until smooth. Spread over cooled bars and allow bars to set before cutting into squares.

Servings: 16

Nutrition Facts

Serving size: 1/16 of a recipe (4.2 ounces).
Percent daily values based on the Reference Daily Intake (RDI) for a 2000 calorie diet.
Nutrition information calculated from recipe ingredients.

Amount Per Serving	
Calories	549.76
Calories From Fat (48%)	262.35
	% Daily Value
Total Fat 31.06g	**48%**
Saturated Fat 14.36g	**72%**
Cholesterol 56.94mg	**19%**
Sodium 190.05mg	**8%**
Potassium 207.14mg	**6%**
Total Carbohydrates 65.2g	**22%**
Fiber 4.18g	**17%**
Sugar 27.92g	
Protein 9.93g	**20%**

ChocoRice Pudding

4		eggs, slightly beaten		4	oz	semisweet chocolate, chopped
2	cups	half-and-half		1/4	cup	packed brown sugar
1/3	cup	granulated sugar		1	Tbs	cornstarch
1/4	cup	unsweetened cocoa powder		1/3	cup	water
1	tsp	vanilla		2	Tbs	chocolate-flavored syrup
1	cup	cooked rice, cooled		1	Tbs	molasses

Procedure

1. Preheat oven to 325°.
2. In a large bowl whisk eggs, half-and-half, sugar, cocoa and vanilla. Stir in rice and chocolate. Pour mixture into a 1 1/2- or 2-quart casserole dish. Place dish in a 13x9 inch baking pan and set on an oven rack. Carefully pour 1-inch of boiling water into the baking pan.
3. Bake, uncovered, for 60 to 65 minutes or until a knife inserted near center comes out clean.
4. Stir together brown sugar and cornstarch in a saucepan. Stir in water, chocolate syrup and molasses. Cook and stir mixture over medium-low heat for 2 minutes more or until thickened and bubbly.
5. To serve, spoon warm pudding into bowls. Pour 1 to 2 tablespoons sauce over each serving.

Servings: 8

Nutrition Facts

Serving size: 1/8 of a recipe (5.8 ounces).
Percent daily values based on the Reference Daily Intake (RDI) for a 2000 calorie diet.
Nutrition information calculated from recipe ingredients.

Amount Per Serving	
Calories	309.72
Calories From Fat (42%)	129.69
	% Daily Value
Total Fat 15.11g	**23%**
Saturated Fat 8.2g	**41%**
Cholesterol 145.15mg	**48%**
Sodium 89.12mg	**4%**
Potassium 251.73mg	**7%**
Total Carbohydrates 39.72g	**13%**
Fiber 2.31g	**9%**
Sugar 19.63g	
Protein 7.41g	**15%**

Fall Fruit Salad

2	Red Delicious apples		1	cup	vanilla yogurt
1	Granny Smith apple		1	tsp	cinnamon
2	Bartlett pears		1/4 tsp		ground ginger
1	sliced banana		1/2 tsp		nutmeg
1/2 lb	seedless red grapes		1	Tbs	apple cider
1/2 cup almond slivers, toasted (optional)					

Procedure

1. Wash and core apples and pears, peeling if desired. Cut into one-inch chunks. Slice bananas ½ inch thick. Wash grapes and cut in half.
2. Combine fruits and almonds in salad bowl. Mix yogurt with spices and cider. Pour over fruit salad and stir to coat fruits evenly. Chill.

Servings: 6

Nutrition Facts

Serving size: 1/6 of a recipe (8 ounces).
Percent daily values based on the Reference Daily Intake (RDI) for a 2000 calorie diet.
Nutrition information calculated from recipe ingredients.

Amount Per Serving	
Calories	150.65
Calories From Fat (5%)	7.76
	% Daily Value
Total Fat 0.9g	1%
Saturated Fat 0.45g	2%
Cholesterol 2.04mg	<1%
Sodium 29.18mg	1%
Potassium 383.68mg	11%
Total Carbohydrates 36.03g	12%
Fiber 4.28g	17%
Sugar 26.68g	
Protein 2.95g	6%

Grapefruit Parfait

2		medium Texas Red Grapefruit	2	6-ounce cartons of your favorite low-fat yogurt
1	cup	granola (with almonds)		(vanilla, banana or strawberry yogurt.)

Procedure

1 Section grapefruit.

2 To assemble parfaits, place about 3 tablespoons grapefruit in each of 4 parfait glasses.

3 Spoon about 1 to 1 1/2 tablespoons yogurt over grapefruit.

4 Sprinkle 2 tablespoons granola over yogurt.

5 Repeat layering until parfait glass is full.

6 Serve immediately.

Servings: 4

Nutrition Facts

Serving size: ¼ of recipe.
Percent daily values based on the Reference Daily Intake (RDI) for a 2000 calorie diet.
Nutrition information calculated from recipe ingredients.

Amount Per Serving	
Calories	259.93
Calories From Fat (24%)	62.92
	% Daily Value
Total Fat 7.15g	11%
Saturated Fat 1.85g	9%
Cholesterol 7.19mg	2%
Sodium 92.88mg	4%
Potassium 555.3mg	16%
Total Carbohydrates 40.65g	14%
Fiber 3.45g	14%
Sugar 19.68g	
Protein 10.56g	21%

Healthy Banana Bread

Incredible taste and texture. For a little chocolate surprise, through in some chocolate chips. If you like a lot of banana, add another banana — t won't hurt!

1/3 cup	vegetable oil (you may substitute 1/3 cup unsweetened applesauce)	1/2 tsp	salt
1/2 cup	honey	1 tsp	baking soda
1 tsp	vanilla extract	1/4 cup	hot water
2	eggs	1/4 tsp	cinnamon
1 1/4	cup mashed bananas (about 3 bananas)	1/2 cup	chopped walnuts (optional)
1 3/4	cups whole wheat flour		

Procedure

1. Preheat oven to 325°.
2. In a large bowl, beat oil and honey together. Add eggs and mix well. Stir in bananas and vanilla. Stir in flour and salt. Add baking soda to hot water; stir to mix and then add to batter. Blend in chopped nuts. Spread batter into a greased 9x5 inch loaf pan.
3. Bake for 55 to 60 minutes. Cool on wire rack for 1/2 hour before slicing.

Servings: 12

Nutrition Facts

Serving size: 1/12 of a recipe (2.9 ounces).
Percent daily values based on the Reference Daily Intake (RDI) for a 2000 calorie diet.
Nutrition information calculated from recipe ingredients.

Amount Per Serving	
Calories	228.95
Calories From Fat (39%)	89.73
	% Daily Value
Total Fat 10.32g	**16%**
Saturated Fat 1.04g	**5%**
Cholesterol 35.25mg	**12%**
Sodium 214.85mg	**9%**
Potassium 144.2mg	**4%**
Total Carbohydrates 31.72g	**11%**
Fiber 1.48g	**6%**
Sugar 14.75g	
Protein 3.97g	**8%**

Marionberry Crisp

This juicy and highly flavored crisp becomes thicker upon cooling. Delicious served with vanilla ice cream or frozen yogurt.

1	cup	rolled oats	1/2 cup	butter or margarine	
1	cup	brown sugar	6	cups	whole Marionberries, fresh, frozen or canned
3/4 cup		flour, divided			

Procedure

1 Preheat oven to 350°.

2 Combine oats, brown sugar and 1/2 cup flour. Cut in butter with pastry blender or two knives until well blended and moist enough to form a ball.

3 Place well drained berries in bottom of 8x8 baking dish and toss with remaining 1/4 cup flour. Sprinkle crumb mixture evenly over fruit and bake in 350° oven for 35-40 minutes or until golden brown.

Servings: 6

Nutrition Facts

Serving size: 1/6 of a recipe.
Percent daily values based on the Reference Daily Intake (RDI) for a 2000 calorie diet.
Nutrition information calculated from recipe ingredients.

Amount Per Serving	
Calories	512.73
Calories From Fat (30%)	155.03
	% Daily Value
Total Fat 17.75g	**27%**
Saturated Fat 10.07g	**50%**
Cholesterol 40.67mg	**14%**
Sodium 18.68mg	**<1%**
Potassium 472.82mg	**14%**
Total Carbohydrates 83.99g	**28%**
Fiber 10.97g	**44%**
Sugar 46.65g	
Protein 8.4g	**17%**

Oatmeal Peanut Butter Cookies

1 1/2	cups	butter	3	cups quick cooking oats
1 1/2	cups	peanut butter	2	cups whole wheat flour
2	cups	packed brown sugar	2	tsp baking soda
3		eggs	1	tsp salt
2	tsp	vanilla extract		

Procedure

1. Preheat oven to 350°.
2. In a mixing bowl, cream the shortening and peanut butter. Add the brown sugar, eggs and vanilla; mix well.
3. Combine oats, flour, baking soda, and salt; add to the creamed mixture and mix well.
4. Drop by rounded teaspoonfuls onto ungreased baking sheet. Flatten with fork. Bake for 12 minutes or until done.

Servings: 24

Nutrition Facts

Serving size: 1/24 of a recipe (2.7 ounces).
Percent daily values based on the Reference Daily Intake (RDI) for a 2000 calorie diet.
Nutrition information calculated from recipe ingredients.

Amount Per Serving	
Calories	348.32
Calories From Fat (53%)	183.08
	% Daily Value
Total Fat 21.23g	**33%**
Saturated Fat 9.32g	**47%**
Cholesterol 61.17mg	**20%**
Sodium 295.48mg	**12%**
Potassium 258.04mg	**7%**
Total Carbohydrates 35.18g	**12%**
Fiber 3.13g	**13%**
Sugar 19.42g	
Protein 7.82g	**16%**

Peanut Rounds

Note: Do not eat these if you are sensitive to nuts.

1		egg, beaten	3	cups	quick cooking rolled oats
1	cup	honey	1	cup	whole wheat flour
1/4 cup		water	3/4 cup		wheat germ
1	tsp	salt	1	cup	peanut pieces
1	tsp	vanilla	2	Tbs	sunflower seeds
3/4 cup		oil (or 3/4 cup unsweetened natural applesauce)			

Procedure

1. Preheat oven to 350°. In bowl, combine egg, honey, water, vanilla and oil. In another bowl, stir together oats, flour and wheat germ. Add liquid mixture to dry ingredients; mix well. Stir in peanut pieces and sunflower seeds. Drop dough from tsp onto a cookie sheet sprayed with cooking spray. Flatten a little.
2. Bake at 350° for 15 to 20 minutes.

Servings: 12

Nutrition Facts

Serving size: 1/12 of a recipe (3.5 ounces).
Percent daily values based on the Reference Daily Intake (RDI) for a 2000 calorie diet.
Nutrition information calculated from recipe ingredients.

Amount Per Serving	
Calories	419.32
Calories From Fat (46%)	192.34
	% Daily Value
Total Fat 22.16g	34%
Saturated Fat 3.15g	16%
Cholesterol 17.63mg	6%
Sodium 202.6mg	8%
Potassium 180.73mg	5%
Total Carbohydrates 50.51g	17%
Fiber 4.05g	16%
Sugar 24.31g	
Protein 9.03g	18%

Pear Bread Pudding

12	oz	sturdy multigrain bread, cut into 1-inch cubes	2 ¾ cups		1 percent low-fat milk
1	Tbs	unsalted butter	2		eggs, lightly beaten
2	Tbs	canola oil	3	Tbs	firmly packed light brown sugar
3		large, firm yet ripe pears, peeled, halved, cored and thinly sliced	2	Tbs	dark honey
			2	tsp	vanilla extract
2	pinches	allspice	1	tsp	ground cinnamon
			1/8 tsp		ground cloves

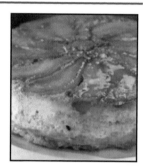

Procedure

1. Preheat oven to 350°. Lightly coat a 9-inch square baking dish with cooking spray.
2. Arrange the bread cubes in a single layer on a baking sheet. Bake until lightly toasted, about 5 minutes. Set aside.
3. In a large, nonstick frying pan, melt 1 ½ teaspoons of the butter over medium heat until bubbly. Stir in 1 tablespoon of the canola oil. Add half of the pear slices to the pan and sauté until evenly browned, about 10 minutes. Sprinkle a generous pinch of allspice onto the pears, and then transfer them to a plate. Repeat with the remaining butter, oil, pears and allspice.
4. Arrange half of the toasted bread cubes evenly in the bottom of prepared baking dish. Top with half of the sautéed pears and then the remaining bread cubes.
5. In a large bowl, combine milk, eggs, 2 tablespoons of the sugar, the honey, vanilla, cinnamon and cloves. Whisk until well blended. Pour the milk mixture over the bread and cover with plastic wrap. Let stand for 20 to 30 minutes, pressing down gently every so often until the bread absorbs the milk mixture. Remove the plastic wrap and arrange remaining pears on top. Sprinkle with remaining 1 tablespoon sugar.
6. Bake until a knife inserted into the center of the pudding comes out clean, 45 to 55 minutes. Let cool for 10 minutes before serving.

Servings: 8

Nutrition Facts

Serving size: 1/8 of a recipe (7.7 ounces).
Percent daily values based on the Reference Daily Intake (RDI) for a 2000 calorie diet.
Nutrition information calculated from recipe ingredients.

Amount Per Serving	
Calories	279.13
Calories From Fat (27%)	76.56
	% Daily Value
Total Fat 8.71g	13%
Saturated Fat 2.43g	12%
Cholesterol 60.89mg	20%
Sodium 264.84mg	11%
Potassium 328.39mg	9%
Total Carbohydrates 43.41g	14%
Fiber 4.84g	19%
Sugar 24.25g	
Protein 8.94g	18%

Raspberry Peach Crisp

2 ½ cups fresh raspberries

4 fresh peaches, pitted and chopped

2/3 cup white sugar, divided

2 Tbs lemon juice

2 pinches cinnamon

1 1/3 cup rolled oats

1/2 cup unsalted butter

1/3 cup brown sugar

1 ½ tsp vanilla extract

1 tsp salt

1 pinch cinnamon

Procedure

1. Preheat oven to 350°. Lightly grease an 8x8 baking dish.

2. In a bowl, mix the raspberries, peaches, lemon juice, 1/3 cup white sugar and 1 pinch cinnamon. In a separate bowl, mix the oats, butter, brown sugar, 1/3 cup white sugar, vanilla, salt and 1 pinch cinnamon.

3. Fill the baking dish with raspberry and peach mixture, and top with oats mixture. Bake 35 minutes in preheated oven, until crisp and golden brown. Cool 10 minutes before serving.

Servings: 6

Nutrition Facts

Serving size: 1/6 of a recipe (6.9 ounces).
Percent daily values based on the Reference Daily Intake (RDI) for a 2000 calorie diet.
Nutrition information calculated from recipe ingredients.

Amount Per Serving	
Calories	391.05
Calories From Fat (39%)	150.66
	% Daily Value
Total Fat 17.18g	26%
Saturated Fat 9.96g	50%
Cholesterol 40.67mg	14%
Sodium 395.11mg	16%
Potassium 257.2mg	7%
Total Carbohydrates 59.12g	20%
Fiber 6.16g	25%
Sugar 42.42g	
Protein 3.62g	7%

Recipe Index

8/14

CPSIA information can be obtained
at www.ICGtesting.com
Printed in the USA
LVIC04n1412040814
397443LV00003B/7